UKRAINE

CIRCUS ART HISTORY

Trauma Therapy for Children

By Lesa Melnyczuk

Copyright ©Lesa Melnyczuk 2025

The information contained in this book is provided for general informational and educational purposes only. While every effort has been made to ensure accuracy and reliability at the time of publication, the author and publisher make no representations or warranties regarding the completeness, reliability, or suitability of the information, products, services, or related graphics contained herein.

This book is not intended to substitute professional advice. Readers are encouraged to seek appropriate professional guidance for their individual circumstances before making any decisions based on the content of this book. The author and publisher expressly disclaim any responsibility for any liability, loss, or risk, personal or otherwise, incurred as a consequence, directly or indirectly, from the use and application of any information contained in this publication.

All rights reserved. No part of this publication may be reproduced, stored in a retrieval system, or transmitted in any form or by any means, electronic, mechanical, photocopying, recording or otherwise, without the prior written permission of the Publisher.

Lesa Melnyczuk (author and creator)
Circus Art History: Trauma Therapy for Children

ISBN 978-1-7636346-9-5 (print)
ISBN 978-1-7641862-0-9 (ebook)

Editing: Mrs Maria Hosja

For more information or to contact the author, please visit: www.lesamelnyczuk.com

CONTENTS

Foreword .... Page 1

Introduction .... Page 7

Chapter One: A Short History of Circus .... Page 11

Chapter Two: The Origins of Circus In Ukraine .... Page 22

Chapter Three: The Independent Ukrainian Circus .... Page 27

Chapter Four: Ukraine's Cultural Ministry .... Page 57

Chapter Five: Circus Arts in Conflict Zones .... Page 61

Chapter Six: Power of Circus in Ukraine .... Page 67

Chapter Seven: Circus as Resistance to Oppression .... Page 69

Chapter Eight: Trauma Recovery & Circus Arts Therapy .... Page 72

Chapter Nine: Circus Schools and Academies .... Page 81

Chapter Ten: International Support & Touring Programs .... Page 87

Chapter Eleven: Overseas Circus Companies .... Page 95

Chapter Twelve: How to become a Circus Performer .... Page 104

Conclusion: 'Circus is alive in Ukraine' .... Page 107

Author's Note .... Page 108

Other Books By Lesa Melnyczuk .... Page 110

References .... Page 111

Author Bio .... Page 122

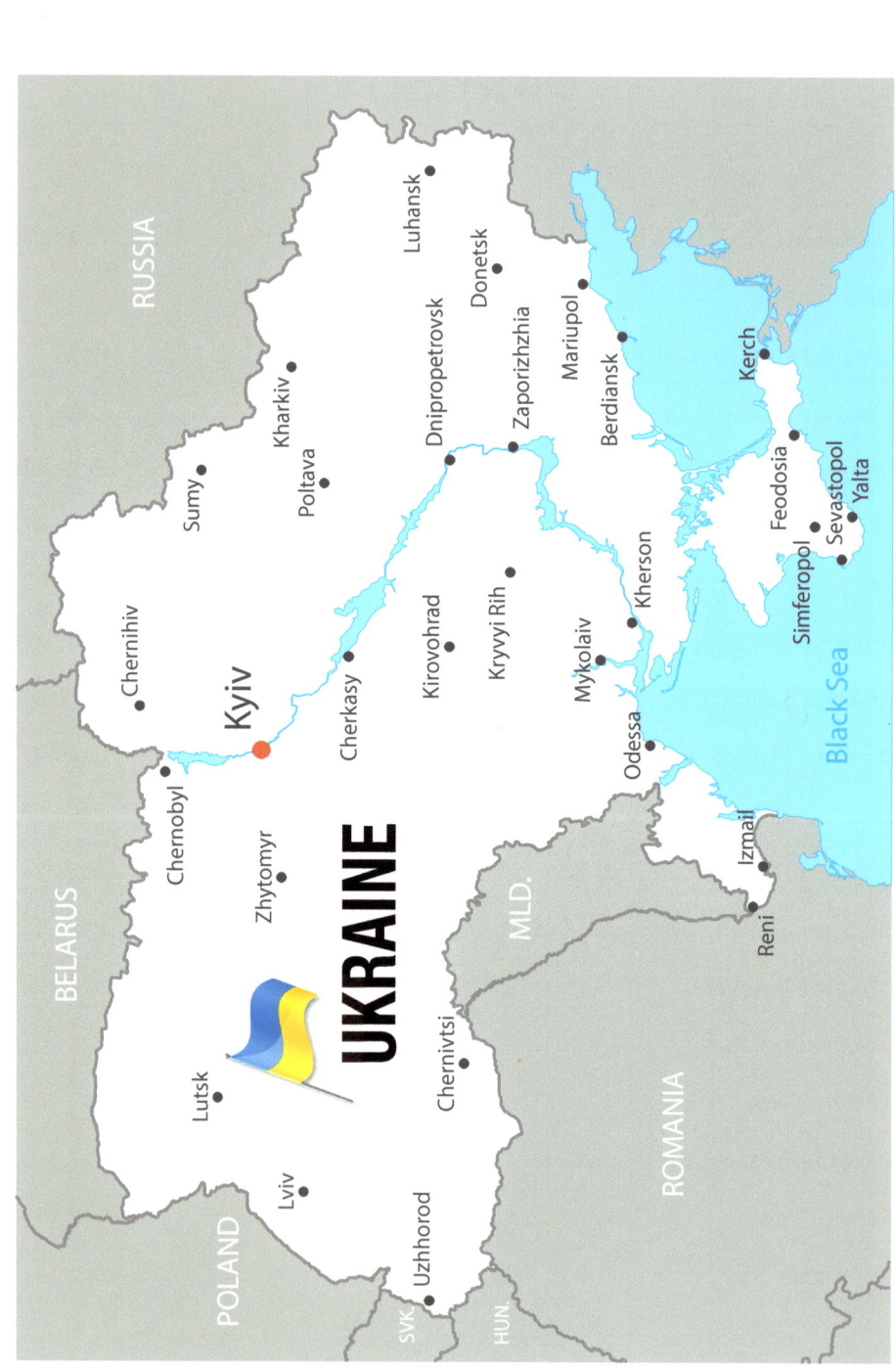

FORWARD

Since the onset of the full-scale war in 2022, millions of Ukrainian children have faced displacement, loss, and psychological trauma. In the middle of this devastation, a surprising lifeline has emerged

the circus.

Far more than entertainment, the circus has become a powerful tool of psychosocial support, creative healing, and cultural continuity for Ukraine's children.

"Amid constant alerts, city bombings, and war news, the acrobat finds balance, the clown continues to bring laughter and joy, and the aerial gymnast risks health and life while performing stunts under the circus dome… Under such conditions, circus art transforms into something more than simply 'the art of wonder.' It gains a unique meaning and depth.

The art our performers create today becomes an open manifesto of the strength, will, and spirit of the Ukrainian people and each individual who serves a noble purpose. It is both beautiful and courageous. Our exhibition is about light in dark times".

(Sydorenko, 2024)

Words of Maksym Sydorenko, editor of *CircusLife.com.ua and author of the stories,* **The Photo Exhibition Ukrainian Circus During the War.**

The exhibition photographer, Circus Life's Nikita Deliukov, selected just 21 photos to capture the experience of Ukrainian circus artists. He found the task extremely difficult.

National Circus Director Vladyslav Korniienko emphasizes the exhibition's importance in illustrating the truth about the war:

"The world must know the truth about the war, about the Ukrainian circus, and about circus artists whose lives are threatened daily by Russian missiles. We sincerely hope this exhibition reaches as many European cities as possible. Please understand that Ukraine is today the defender of European civilization, and we need your support.

Help us preserve Ukrainian culture and circus, both integral parts of Europe's cultural life. We hope for the swift end of the war and look forward to shared projects".
(Sydorenko, 2024)

The Exhibition was held in Berlin during October/November then followed by Kyiv in December, 2024

"The world must know the truth about the war, about the Ukrainian circus, and about circus artists whose lives are threatened daily by Russian missiles. We sincerely hope this exhibition reaches as many European cities as possible. Please understand that Ukraine is today the defender of European civilization…
(Maksym Sydorenko, editor of CircusLife.com.ua)

The images of Ukraine's Circus art in wartime conditions are a profound testament to the resilience of Ukrainians and their dedication to circus art. It officially opened in December 2024 in Shevchenko Park near the Taras Shevchenko monument. Taras Shevchenko is Ukraine's most celebrated and well-known iconic Ukrainian poet, writer, artist and political figure. This exhibition is a project by Circus Life, a Ukrainian media outlet focussing on circus arts, showcasing the beauty and significance of circus art in Ukraine. Even in wartime it holds a very important place. (Sholokhova, 2024)

INTRODUCTION

At a time when the world for many Ukrainian children has become a place of fear, unpredictability and tragically, death, the circus offers a welcome counterbalance: laughter, rhythm, distraction, community, challenge and wonder.

When Chris Mayhew, an experienced former circus performer and teacher from Perth Western Australia went to Ukraine for nine days to visit a colleague and observe their circus training, he stayed for three months, such was the fascinating circus experience he witnessed in wartime Ukraine.

Chris is the owner of the Circus Centre in Bibra lake and was invited to visit the State- funded Alle-Up Circus School in Kyiv, directed by head Coach Oleh Kurinskyi. This had been organised before Russia invaded Ukraine in 2022. It was not until September 2024 that he was able to take some time off and travel to Ukraine, despite the ongoing war. (Hiatt B, 2025)

The article in a local newspaper describing his visit to Ukraine, captured my interest and, I made contact.

Chris was interviewed during his visit in Ukraine and painted a 'striking picture of the differences between the circus landscapes of Australia and Ukraine.' In Perth with approximately 200 recreational students, he observed how different Ukrainian circus training was. His words were: 'It is more intense and students dedicating 4 to 5 days a week to their circus art training.' Chris noted that the 'level of skill and artistry surpasses anything he's witnessed in Australia.' Chris noted 'admiration for the discipline and passion of young Ukrainian performers' was palpable. Chris learned what Ukrainians have known for decades, that the tradition of circus in Ukraine is 'not merely a pastime but a respected art form with a clear professional pathway.' (Sidorenko, 2024) By contrast circus students in Perth may train for only four hours per week.

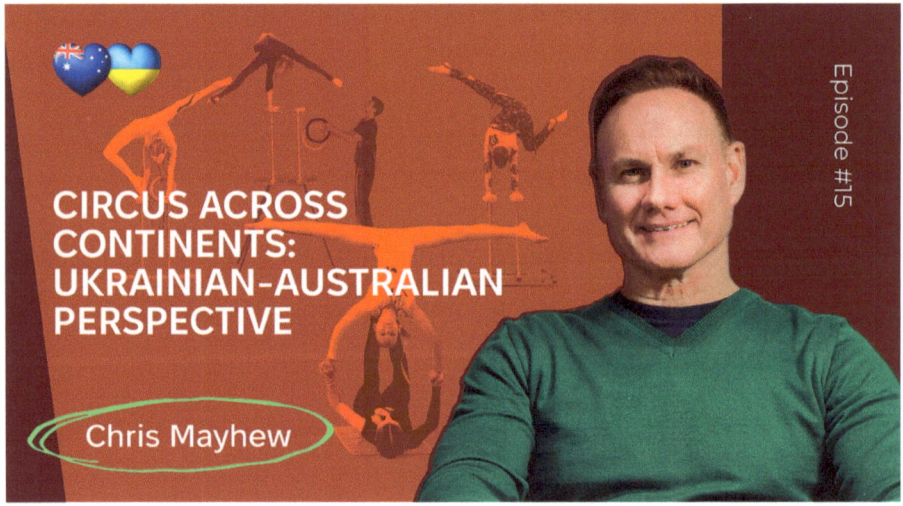

My contact with Chris resulted in an afternoon event for our local Ukrainian refugee children who migrated to Perth Western Australia escaping the Russian invasion. Chris opened his Circus School for two hours on a Saturday afternoon to give our newest arrivals a taste of an experience that they understood more so than their west Australian counterparts might have. Circus in Ukraine is a revered art form. (Hiatt, *2025*)

The notion that Ukrainian children facing trauma from Russia's invasion were still training hard in Circus in Ukraine, was extraordinary and piqued my interest.

And so apart from arranging a free experience for our newest Ukrainian refugee children in Perth, I envisaged a book about Circus in Ukraine touching on Ukrainian's fight and her ever suffering children were not being forgotten.

As a child I remember attending shows in Perth whenever a travelling Circus came to town. I remember the animals, circus performers and clowns. The big circular tent would be erected on a large, grassed area of our town's foreshore, the show would be advertised for some weeks and be full to capacity, with excited families. I remembered my own experience, the smell of the animals, sawdust, the trailers, the brightly coloured printing on the sides. The tent seemed huge at the time with the tiered benches where we took up position. Such excitement and fear watching aerialists and at times, animals performing.

However, when I watched a short film taken by Chris of the Ukrainian children performing in Kyiv, I saw Circus on a completely elevated level. Circus, in Ukraine and Europe per se, is a very highly developed and respected art form. It is recognised as highly artistic, professional and an integral part of Ukraine's Arts heritage.

And so I began research for something so uniquely linked to the situation in Ukraine resulting from the invasion by Russia from February 2022.

This book is my way of raising awareness of a remarkable country, an homage my heritage and one integral part of Ukraine's culture, a culture that is at the heart of my Ukrainian soul.

History of Circus

Where do we begin writing about Circus in Ukraine? How can we link it up to what we in Australia understand as Circus?

I decided that a short core understanding of the concept of circus and the beginning of circus, followed briefly by examining the history of circus, both in Ukraine and then also Australia, would be a way forward.

This book is not a comprehensive outline or history of Circus anywhere, only a *brief taster* of the history of Circus evolution in Ukraine and Australia.

There is no intention to make comparisons between Ukraine and Australia for that is impossible, given the two contemporary circus histories. However, Australia is my birthplace, and Ukrainian heritage is my birthright, thus I was interested in looking at the two distinctly different circus histories, attitudes and developments of circus as an art.

Although beginning as a penal colony, Australia has not faced war as such, certainly never such massive historical invasions as Ukraine has suffered a few times. As a borderland, Ukraine has had a long history of aggression. The word 'Ukraine' actually translates as 'border land (Ukraina -ookrayina).' The territory faced many border changes until finally becoming independent in 1991. Australia is surrounded by water and thus enjoys a semblance of protection by distance as well.

CHAPTER 1

The term 'circus' as a noun is defined by Google's English Dictionary. (Google,2025)

"a travelling company of acrobats, clowns, and other entertainers which gives performances, typically in a large tent, in a series of different places:"

"I was thrilled by the annual visits of the circus:"

"a large group of people travelling together on the circuit of a particular high-profile activity:"

"The Formula One grand prix circus:"

"a public scene of frenetic, noisy, or confused activity:" "a media circus:" or,

"(in ancient Rome) a rounded or oval arena lined with tiers of seats, used for equestrian and other sports and games:"

"The Circus Maximus:"

"(British) a rounded open space in a town or city where several streets converge;" "Piccadilly Circus."

1.1 A Short History of Circus

The origin of circus began in Ancient Rome, in a roofless open-air arena for the exhibition of horse and chariot races, equestrian shows, staged battles, gladiatorial combat, and displays of (and fights with) trained animals.

In ancient Rome, a circus (the Latin word meaning "circle") also hosted other events like wild animal hunts, gladiator fights, and public executions. The most famous Roman circus was the Circus Maximus, which could hold an estimated 150,000 to 250,000 spectators." (Wikipedia, 2025)

The Roman circus ran chariot races, one of the most popular of ancient Greek, Roman, and Byzantine sports. Although sometimes the 'circus' served other purposes. It was similar to the ancient Greek hippodrome, theatres and amphitheatres. Circuses were one of the main entertainment venues at the time. (Wikipedia, 2025)

The largest and most renowned circus was Circus Maximus constructed in the 6th century BCE Rome, Italy. According to Edward Gibbon in 1776, it may have existed in some form from as early as around 500 BC. Circuses were mainly constructed during the 400 years between 200 BC and 200 AD. The Circus Maximus was a chariot racetrack in Rome which was also used for other events such as the Roman Games and gladiator fights. (Gibbon, 1776)

The early Roman circus histories were extensive and are better examined separately in other comprehensive publications should you want more depth. It is not my intention to provide a comprehensive history in this publication although some material will be covered.

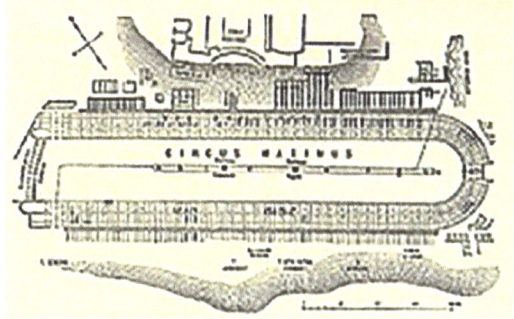

Partially excavated in the 20th century and then remodelled, today it continues as an important public space, hosting music concerts and rallies. See below.

Illustration by Mark Cartwright*, 12 June 2013*

https://www.worldhistory.org/image/1276/circus-maximus-present-day/

1.2 The beginning of the modern circus: The United Kingdom

The modern circus was evident from 1978 in London, with trick horsemanship. It was held in a field called Ha'penny Patch at Lambeth on the southern side of the Thames.

Sergeant-Major Philip Astley, a former cavalryman and Seven Years War veteran developed combined acts with horsemanship, clown acts, ropewalkers, tumblers and gymnasts in this circular area. It was called Astley's Amphitheatre, after him, Sergeant- Major Philip Astley. (2021, St Leon)

This new type of entertainment became known around London as 'The Circus.' Thus began the large open-air circular riding tracks used by recreational riders. These tracks remain as thoroughfares nowadays. Piccadilly Circus in London is one. Two different evolving circus developments.

There is no specific evolutionary link seen by Valentine St Leon to the Roman Circus. Astley's remained famous from 1825-1841 with equestrian/horse-based pantomimes and spectacles that were imitated throughout the UK, on the Continent, in the USA and of course, Australia. (2010, St Leon)

It was Astley who was credited with deciding that the ideal size for a circus ring is 42 feet in diameter. This was the best size that enabled him to use centrifugal force to help balance on a horse's back while riding fast around a ring. The performer rode at speed around the ring, the gravity was used to push him onto the horse's back and so it preventing him from falling onto the sawdust floor.

In the late eighteenth-century England the first generations of circus performers emerged. Most performers came from underprivileged backgrounds. If they committed a lawful offence and were charged, they were transported/relocated to Australia. They began the start of Circus in Australia as an industry, with such entertainments until the early 1930s. Interestingly the years of famine genocide , the Holodomor by Stalin in Ukraine.

This is an interior view of Astley's Royal Amphitheatre, unknown maker, 19th century, London. © Victoria and Albert Museum, London

A performance by two ropewalkers in Sydney 1833, was held in the new theatre Royal building. It was said to be a sensational public performance!

There were few performers travelling from London or the Continent before the golden rushes of the 1950s. This changed over time.

Circus as an art lets us create something that is physical and full of emotion. It is used to entertain, perform and bring happiness and laughter to people. It is often said it can raise the spirit of an audience.

There are many publications discussing the development of the modern Circus. In this publication I have sourced some that will outline a simple development for understanding. Again, it is not a complete history but a taster if you like with a simple focus on Ukraine.

The story of circus · V&A Victoria and Albert,2025. The V&A holds in its collection a large number of objects that reveal the fascinating history of the circus. 28/04/20

Https://www.vam.ac.ul/articles/the-story-of-circus?srsltid=AfB...

1.3 The American Circus

Circus had spread throughout Europe but also found its way to the US. 1793 saw John Rickets whose expertise as a Scottish horse rider, was trick horse riding. His exhibitions included rope walkers, the usual tumblers, pantomimes and the necessary clown.

These began in Philadelphia and New York City. He and his horse, Cornplanter were the first animal performers. John Durang is known to be the first American born clown.

As we know every circus needed a "ringmaster" to keep the horses running properly in the ring with performing riders. The ringmaster eventually took on the role of an MC and they continue to wear the traditional riding outfit.

The Ringmaster had a very important role in, not only performing, but calling out and introducing the performers.

The Royal Hanneford Circus has been called the oldest circus in the world. It is an American-based touring family circus which began in 1690. The family first performed as a traveling troupe in 1807, but it is believed that the family performed separately

https://en.wikipedia.org › wiki › Ringmaster_(circus)

through the United Staes during the early 20th century. (29/04/2025, Royal Hanneford Circus) *https://en.wikipedia.org/wiki/Royal_Hanneford_Circus*

Edwin "Poodles" Hanneford (1891-1967), the patriarch was seen as one of the greatest trick horse riders in history. He performed the first somersault from one running horse to another. He held a Guinness Book of World Records record for 26 running jumps on and off a horse 26 times in a row. It was a huge feat of agility.

Still from No Loafing (1923) with Poodles Hanneford and Joe Roberts
https://en.wikipedia.org/wiki/Royal_Hanneford_Circu

One of the worst calamites that could befall a circus was a fire. Like Ashley's Circus, Rickets circus experienced a fire in New York. After another burnt to the ground and becoming bankrupt, Rickets decided to travel to England and reestablish a circus career there. Unfortunately, the ship on which he was sailing, perished at sea and everyone on board drowned.

The growth of the circus tradition with animal performers began. Some were almost full travelling zoos. However, contained within two or three wagons and performing now in the circus tent called a "big top."

The next circus US development was with an elephant "Old Bet" that was owned by Hackaliah Bailey of New York. Old Bet was a young elephant calf. Probably taken from her family on the African plains and finding herself on the US circus circuit. She was touring a country that was not familiar to her, and probably confused by her different life away from family and herd for the entertainment of people loving circus and seeing unfamiliar animals. Old Bet lived until July 1816. She was shot dead near Maine by local farmer Daniel Davis. An award winning animated film about her called "The Elephant's Song" directed by Lynn Tomlinson.

The work to get elephants out of circuses began in 1980. It was considered cruel to keep these animals in such confinement.

And so the US became a world leader in Circus developments. They became bigger and more extravagant adding larger tents and added unique trapeze skills performances.

A partnership of T. Barnum and James A. Bailey lasted a century in the development of the 'Great International Circus.' Their main competitors in the late 19th century was The Ringling Brothers founded in 1884. They were essentially based on weather and retired during the winter months to rest and reset for another performing period. They would work on the standard events such as the parades, acts of circus skills, animal performances and the clown acts. The parade was the beginning of the circus coming to town. It became traditional. These parades were spectacular with caravans that were richly decorated.

And so the circus developed over the years and the circus culture evolved into what it is today. From such diverse beginnings we see the development of a more sophisticated circus culture and act today.

1.4. Circus Culture

The concept of 'circus' culture or art as a meaningful and defining characteristic of human life and society, is not particularly easy to grasp by most people with no experience of or connection, to it.

The concept 'culture' is applied to diverse areas of human activity such as education, training, and striving for human perfection, regarding a person's intellectual and practical proclivity. Circus is one of those forms of human activity that is also divided into a more intellectual form of art. Something transcending physical activity has evolved over time.

'The most common classification of such art is that which is based on artistic means of human expressiveness. It belongs to one of the main kinds of art, and that is choreographic art including dance, circus and pantomime.' (Sukhomlynsky, 2022i) From this we see the evolution and the notion that, the literal circus arts are still alive in Ukraine, despite the ongoing war and hardship. Ukrainian circus performers, companies, and schools have shown incredible resilience, continuing to perform, train, and even tour internationally. Some performers have entered competitions such as Britain's got Talent and always wowed the crowd and judges. Many people worldwide have watched Cirque de Soleil perform. This company has a history of involving Ukrainian Circus performers. Ukraine has a long and respected tradition of circus arts. It has become a respected and revered performance art.

Circus skills remind people/children that their bodies can still move freely. They reaffirm, that trust can be rebuilt. We all remember falling off logs or 'monkey bars' as children and understanding that we can keep doing it and master the skill after countless falls, cuts and at times, physical injuries. Circus skills remind people/children that such actions, our stories - even painful ones - can be revisited and told with courage and colour through such a unique physical art. These skills have developed over decades, through circus schools and training. The history of circus in Ukraine is a fascinating one that begs to be told. Especially now. It has become more than a force of entertainment. It has generated healing during times of uncertainty, loss, injury, death and devastation.

So hopefully you have some basis for the history of circus, the development of circus art and are now curious about circus as an art in Ukraine, and how it has managed to exist through ruin and war assaulting it every day from Russia's invasion of 2022. A unique period in the development and existence of circus schools and academies and the children and teachers devoting their lives and time to keep the flames alive in the hearts of Ukraine's circus performers.

CHAPTER 2

The Origins of Circus In Ukraine

Circus in Ukraine developed in parallel to that of western Europe. Frescoes on religious buildings show images of 'buffoons' (jesters making people laugh) and jugglers, in the early times of Kievan Rus. Singing, acrobats and dancing were the order of the folk theatre.

After the early developments with Astley's established circus in England, circus businessmen began expanding and moving east into Europe into the Russian Empire. Frenchman Jaques Tournier started in St Petersburgh in 1827 and Jean-Baptiste Godefroy built a tent in Odessa.

A temporary wooden circus in Kharkiv (a large city only 30 kilometres from the Russian border) was established by Prussian Wilhelm Sur in 1862 followed by a stone building, Grikke in 1906.

Ignatius Sobbot from Austria built the first stationary circus building in Kyiv in 1875 which closed from Circus but was rented to theatre groups. (Burrow, D., 2024)

The original modern circus was created during Russian times but by western European entrepreneurs looking to make money.

Two poor brothers, Petro and Dmytro Akim, who began as street artists purchased material from the Czech Circus Emmanual

Beranek and, after a Russian premiere in Penza in 1873 they opened buildings in Kyiv, Odessa and Kharkiv. They introduced Ukrainian music and folklore elements into the performances to create a unique and competetive Ukrainian Circus style.

Circus was a privately organised operation during the second half of the 19th and early 20th century. 1917 and the revolution saw Ukraine become a unique entity which brought politics and ideology into the circus world. Soviet authorities took control, and propaganda became a useful tool, sometimes becoming a dangerous double-edged sword.

Post World War II, stationary circuses were built in the Ukrainian Soviet Socialist Republic. Some of these will be included in this book.

As of recent records at the time of composing this material, the following were the prominent state circuses in Ukraine. Some insight will be noted as to whether they are still operational in 2025:

2.1 National Circus of Ukraine (Kyiv)

Established in 1960 and then designated as the national circus in 1998, it serves as the principal circus arena in the country. The venue has a large seating capacity of 2,100 and is renowned for its broadly diverse performances and training programs. Beginning in 2025, the circus presented a cabaret-style show entitled "Circus Rendezvous", which was a blend of traditional and contemporary circus arts. Thus clearly in full operation entertaining Ukrainians. Few tourists while Ukraine is designated unsafe for travel.

2.2 Dnipro State Circus

Opened in 1980, this circus is notable for being the only one in Ukraine equipped with a dedicated rehearsal and production arena. Its auditorium can accommodate 1,914 spectators. The Dnipro State Circus is still operating as of 2025. It still hosts performances and shows such as in March 2025, "Pinocchio: New Adventures."

2.3 Lviv State Circus

The Lviv State Circus officially opened its doors in 1969. This circus has faced operational challenges due to the ongoing conflict in Ukraine. Many cultural institutions in Ukraine have had to suspend or modify their activities to ensure the safety of performers and audiences but the Lviv Circus like others, has not. Apart from a new programme for May 2025. It held a special performance for children and families of the Ukrainian defenders 20 Dec 2024. The Ukrainian summer's circus performances for children whose parents are at the front, demonstrates how important *circuses* are to Ukrainians and Ukrainian life. With a war raging in the east.

2.4 Kharkiv State Circus

Recognized as the oldest circus in Ukraine, it was founded in 1886. The current facility can host over 2,000 attendees and is equipped with modern amenities. Although the Kharkiv State Circus is still said to be operating in 2025, there is no evidence to this author.

2.5 Zaporizhzhia State Circus

A key venue in southeastern Ukraine, inaugurated in 1972, it continues to uphold the region's circus traditions. The Zaporizhzhia State Circus is still in operation as of early 2025. It was struck twice by Russian shelling in 2022 but continued to function and serve its community. Initially it became a hub for internally displaced Ukrainians.

Artists showcase aerial hoop performance at the Zaporizhzhia State Circus, in Zaporizhzhia, Ukraine, on Feb. 11, 2024. (Andriy Andriyenko/SOPA Images/LightRocket via Getty Images)

2.6 Kryvyi Rih State Circus

Opening in 1970 and serving the central Ukrainian city of Kryvyi Rih, this circus contributes significantly to the local cultural landscape. The Kryvyi Rih State Circus is still operating as of 2025. The circus continues to host performances and events. This city is the home of the current President of Ukraine, President Zelenskiy. "Circus on Water Wonderland" is performing in May 2025.

2.7 Donetsk State Circus

Known as "Kosmos" it is currently operating as of February 2025. It had been closed for nearly three years due to regional instability but reopened in late 2024 with the premiere of the show "Империя львиц" ("Empire of Lionesses"). The reopening was supported by the Russian State Circus Company (Rosgostsirk), which has been touring the new Russian occupied regions since the invasion of 2022. All proceeds are directing to support circuses in newly occupied Donetsk and Luhansk.

Kosmos was once a prominent institution in eastern Ukraine. However, due to the ongoing conflict its status is uncertain.

2.8 Simferopol State Circus

Simferopol, the second largest city in Crimea, was annexed by Russia in 2014. Circus was stablished in Crimea in 1959.

Its operations have been affected by the geopolitical changes since 2014. The Circus, officially known as the Simferopol State Circus of Boris Tezikov is still operating in 2025. The circus continues to host performances and events. Albeit under Russian occupation.

CHAPTER 3

The Independent Ukrainian Circus

The collapse of the USSR led to a growth of an independent Ukrainian circus landscape with modern influences from all over the world. After gaining Independence in 1991, the Ministry of Culture of Ukraine took over circus companies located on Ukrainian territory. In 1993 a creative association was set up to preserve and develop Ukrainian national circus art as well as coordinate the activities of the circus industry of Ukraine. It was called 'Ukrderzhtsirk.'

Ukrderzhtsirk' became the 'State Circus Company of Ukraine.'

The 1989/90's economic crisis and declining status of artists in Ukraine resulted in losses of circus job opportunities. That led to Ukrainian circus artists working abroad. That is still the model today. Ukrainian artists are some of the best in the world and can secure work in world renowned companies travelling the world.

2014 saw a turning point when circuses in Ukraine were impacted by the Russian occupation.

The Russian-backed military took over towns and cities in Ukraine's eastern Donbas region. Donetsk People's Republic (DPR) and the Luhansk People's Republic (LPR) were proclaimed as Russian independent, separatist states. This started the Donbas war.

Thus the current war began in February 2014, when Putin seized Crimea and his Russian proxies took over those parts of eastern Ukraine, the rebel states. Putin ordered up to 200,000 soldiers into Ukraine to sweep into the capital, Kyiv, and overthrow the pro- Western government. He wanted to return Ukraine to Russia's 'sphere of influence.' He failed in the attempt and there is still a war raging between the two nations.

Ukrainian culture and identity have in fact existed for centuries independently of Russia but Putin has tried to erase the identity and history of Ukraine with his all-out, indiscriminate destruction of everything be it structural or human. The terror, the bombing, the raping, the killing, the looting, the torture and the general cruel goal of the invasion was essentially to erase the Ukrainian nation.

Ukrainians sought shelter in underground shelters as Russian forces attacked on 24 February 2022. Taken by Marcus Yam/ Los Angeles Times

3.1 Euromaidan

As Putin launched the biggest European invasion since the end of World War Two, he gave a fiery speech on TV declaring his goal was to "demilitarise and denazify" Ukraine.

Russia had been painting modern Ukraine as a Nazi state. It was a huge distortion of history. Eight years earlier Putin had taken over the Ukrainian Crimean Peninsula.

Trouble began in 2013 when Yanukovich withdrew from signing an association agreement with the EU. Russia did not want such an agreement although Ukraine's parliament were overwhelming in their approval to do this. A revolution erupted to get rid of Ukraine's pro- Russian president Victor Yanukovich and replaced him with a more pro-Western government. Some 100 protesters were killed by government forces during the conflict. Yanukovich was removed in the 2014 Revolution of Dignity, the Euromaidan, after huge protests against him. He fled to Russia with the help of Putin and lives there in exile.

The agreement was crucial for the future of Ukraine becoming part of the EU. It began with respect for human rights, freedoms and the rule of law. Political dialogue would involve discussion focussing on political reforms in justice, and security. There was also to be sectoral cooperation with respect to energy, the environment, climate action, transport, agriculture, rural development, consumer protection to name a few major issues. Sectoral partnerships means that different countries work together towards achieving a common goal, sharing resources and responsibilities working towards addressing complex challenges.

Euromaidan - Wikipedia

The Euromaidan protests in Ukraine and the subsequent aftermath, did not directly impact circuses in any significant way. Euromaidan was a political protest, against the government's decision not to sign a political association and free trade agreement with the European Union. This agreement defied Russian domination of that region in the east of Ukraine. Losing any semblance of control over Ukraine was simply unacceptable.

However, when we look at the effect on those circuses located in Russian occupied territories such as Donetsk, Luhansk, Simferopol, Sevastopol and Yalta, it was extreme on all counts.

What followed those disrupted years was the development of private tent circuses. By 2020, there were around 50 such circuses. Unfortunately, the result of private tent circuses was a decline in the artistic quality to a low standard. This then made the situation appear chaotic.

Nevertheless, the National Circus in Kyiv, continued to develop quality performances. The Kyiv circus building continued with regular performances with a change to proceedings. A notice stating *'the show will not have an intermission. Should there be an air raid patrons should leave through the exits and move down to the bomb shelters. The show will continue after 20-30 minutes after the air-raid has ended.'* This procedure continues today in 2025.

With the front on the doorstep for some time and, constant Russian shelling, Kharkiv had to cancel all performances. Many high-quality performers moved overseas, stopped performing and training or are fighting. There are, unfortunately, few circus employment opportunities for these artists.

Many western European circus lovers know Ukrainian artists. They have seen their artistry through Cirque de Soleil and other travelling shows. Unfortunately, though, there are few images of the Ukrainian Circus generally available publicly. Hopefully this book will provide a basic outline and rectify that. You will read how important they were and how valuable they are today.

If we look at some 'beneficial' outcomes of the Russian invasion, there has been an increased exposure of Ukraine as never before, albeit horrific in many instances.

Knowledge and recognition of Ukraine and her culture has never been so widespread and conspicuous, constantly disseminated further through daily television broadcasts and other media. The world is attempting to extrapolate the meaning behind this heinous invasion of a sovereign country by its neighbour.

As a result Circus productions with Ukrainian casts have increased and the Ukrainian circus culture has had a greater exposure throughout Europe. A production called 'Waterland' from the Zaporozhian Circus toured Germany as a tent production, having also been to Poland. It will initially be a water show and then eventually become an ice production. It is still playing and will performed in Ukraine during April and May 2025.

3.2 The National Circus of Ukraine

In 1868, the Frenchman Auguste Bergognie bought land in downtown Kiev. He approached the town council for permission to build a stone building to house a circus.

The first opening of Circus Bergognie took place in 1875. It was one of the earliest permanent circus venues in Kyiv.

Thus, while Circus Bergognie is not the current national circus, it played a foundational role in the development of circus arts in Ukraine.

A more modernised building of the National Circus was designed by architect Valentin Zhukov with 2100 seats. It was inaugurated in 1960. In 1998, the Kiev circus was granted the status of the National Circus of Ukraine. This building is the largest domed building in Kiev city and is considered an important place of not only entertainment but cultural heritage.

The building is considered an architectural marvel in travel publications presenting some inspiring performances both intricate, as well as whimsical clown performances including trained circus animals.

The 1960s and 1979s was an era of Soviet grandeur. It was considered very important to showcase circus culture and artistry for tourists as well as local patrons. High-levels of artistry and spectacle were expected of the acrobats and performers.

The National Circus was able to lure big named international acts and performers from around the world in those early years. Many careers in circus arts were launched in this venue.

Circus artistry changed and grew with contemporary techniques augmenting dance as an artform. Circus skills preserved the traditional elements of circus acts, incorporating circus history with the new developments.

With such changes the Ukrainian circus became a platform for innovation in performing arts. All within an amazing, uniquely designed building with a wonderful dome. Which has aged very little and has only had a few structural renovations over the years.

The interesting aspect to circus in Ukraine is that it retains a strong educational basis. Circus is a respected arts medium in Ukraine, where local schools and courses, incorporate the values of the art and of circus performance within their youth and learning programmes.

Although not commonly recognised in the west for many years, the world now understands the years of trouble Ukraine has suffered at the hands of its neighbours. As a result of Russia's invasion in 2022. Notwithstanding the Stalin era and the forced famine genocide of 1932-1933, which we refer to as the Holodomor. (Melnyczuk, 2018)

NATIONAL CIRCUS OF UKRAINE IN KIEV (2025)
All You MUST Know Before You Go (w/Reviews)

Throughout the challenging years of political and socio-economic problems, Ukraine's Circus was still able to develop amazing shows, rich in artistic creativity. Ukrainian artists continued to showcase their strengths and talents with the very best spiritual soul of their culture. That strength has never wavered, even under terror and constant siege as a nation defending its sovereignty.

3.3 The Kyiv Municipal Academy of Performing and Circus Arts

Founded in 1961 The Academy was an institution that offered students courses in a higher Bachelor's Education or a Master's degree. It was an educational institution where students could graduate with international skills and levels in singing, dancing, acting, producing, and circus arts. These could be in juggling, clowning, gymnastics, acrobatic, pantomime, aerialists, illusion and other related skills.

https://kmaecm.edu.ua/en/history

This is an historical photo of the circus building in Kyiv that was founded in 1961. The Ukrainian National Circus before the Academy was located in the building below.

Many graduates have become stars in world leading circuses and theatres. They have excelled in pop shows and, of course, become celebrities in Ukrainian and European show business.

The Academy's mission is to 'foster artistic excellence, cultivate creativity and provide a comprehensive education in the field of performing and circus arts.' It achieves this by providing students with the skills, knowledge and professionalism for a successful career in performing arts. (Kyiv Municipal Academy of Performing and Circus Arts, n.d. *About the Academy*. Retrieved from *http://example-url.ua)*

The Academy has a well-known alumni. Surprisingly it is still in operation. The war with Russia continues in 2025 at the time of writing this book. There are many internally displaced students and loss of families. However, throughout the devastation, terror, destruction, countless deaths and mayhem, The Academy continues to encourage high levels of artistic excellence and creativity. Chris Mayhew, from Perth in Western Australia and the catalyst for this publication, was to witness the Academy and the magic in action within, first hand.

Images © Kyiv Municipal Academy of Performing and Circus Arts
inbox@kmaecm.edu.ua

Students today can graduate as Theatre Directors; Directors of Theatre, Performing and Circus Arts; as well as become a Circus Director; Choreographer; Manager of Show Business, Masters of Ceremonies and so forth. (KMACPA, 2025)

3.4 The Dnipro Circus

Mobile tent Circuses were popular during the 1800s in Dnipro, until a permanent building was constructed in 1885. The public began supporting its live performances again by 1911 and by 1929 it was relocated to Ozerna square. World War II and Nazi occupation saw the evacuation of the Circus. However, after some changes over time, a completely new structure was built in June 1960. It was designed by V.A. Zhukova, an architect from Kyiv. Unfortunately, with no heating, it was only suitable in warmer months. So again, it was relocated in 1980 to a house on the embankment in the city centre. It saw 'The Carnival Goes Around The World Event,' during which the artists gave the construction workers a very enthusiastic.

The Dnipro Circus has a unique dome arch design pattern. This design makes it quite different because it improves the acoustics in the auditorium. It has been designed with bars to allow artists to attach their equipment easily.

The circus was built using a tent covering made up of 12 prefabricated petals of reinforced concrete pieces, called ferro concrete. This material is low in terms of tercile strength which means the maximum stress the pieces can tolerate before breaking. By embedding steel reinforcing bars in the concrete before it sets, the material becomes stronger to be pulled and stretched.

This was a first for a domestic building of this era. The most up to date lighting and audio equipment was installed in the hall.

The Dnipro State Circus is the only state circus in Ukraine to have a rehearsal and production or stage venue within its structure.

https://commons.wikimedia.org/w/index.php?curid=91492811

As a result of the changing situation with the Russian invasion, it is difficult to find up to date information as to circus operations in 2025. (2025, Wikipedia:Text of the Creative Commons Attribution-ShareAlike 4.0 International License)

It is possible that the Circus's general director and artistic director, Shabatko may still hold the role. During the first year of the Russian invasion, this circus was still holding performances. It also staged "Pinocchio: New Adventures" in March 2025. However, further investigation through ChatGPT, the online search tool stated that:

As of April 2025, the Dnipro State Circus in Ukraine is likely not operational due to ongoing military activity in the region. Dnipro has experienced recent Russian drone and missile strikes, resulting in injuries and damage to civilian infrastructure. These attacks have led to localized blackouts and damage to buildings.

While the Dnipro State Circus is a notable cultural venue in the city, there is no current information confirming its operational status in 2025. Given the security situation and the impact on civilian infrastructure, it is plausible that the circus has suspended performances or operations. [WikipediaRadioFreeEurope/RadioLibertyLinkedIn](#)

3.5 Old Circus The Grikke Circus_ MSTYSLAV CHERNOV

In the east of Ukraine the major city of Kharkiv has a long circus history which began with the construction of a temporary wooden circus by Prussian Wilhelm Sur in 1862. This was followed in 1906 by Heinrich Grikke, a German merchant and entrepreneur who founded the Grikke circus. There is little specific information but the Grikke seems to have been built by Khrustalev (Pyotr Alekseevich Khrustalev?). Should this be correct then this person is an interesting character himself. He was the first chairman of the St. Petersburg Council of Workers' Deputies from October to November 1905. (retrieved from [ttps://en.wikipedia.org/wiki/Georgy_Stepanovich_Khrustalev-Nosar](https://en.wikipedia.org/wiki/Georgy_Stepanovich_Khrustalev-Nosar))

Grikke was built of stone during the Russian Empire. The building is concealed by many narrow industrial streets but although it looks abandoned it is still a major Circus teaching institution.

Grikke settled in Kharkiv, which was then part of the Russian Empire. Grikke's building was one of the first permanent stone circus buildings in the Russian empire. His German heritage was quite common at the time, as many ethnic Germans lived and worked across the entire Russian Empire. These people contributed to commerce, architecture, and cultural development in Ukraine. They arrived to develop businesses and make money.

"Old Circus" building with its metallic copula. A copula is a dome on the roof of a building. The image above is of the old Grikke Circus building. (Chernov Documentary, 2010-2013)

Circus Grikke, right, as it is today, completely hidden within the old streets of Kharkiv. Although old and with only a few renovations, the Grikke building is still in use, primarily for Circus rehearsals and training. Although much of it needs repair, the building still has the last authentic sawdust arena in Europe. The cupola is still the original. It was never renovated and has a unique roof with unmatched acoustics. According to Chernov, sections are 'closed off due to structural issues like holes in walls, missing floors, and a lack of heating.' The original, only change room, is still in use. (Chernov, 2010-2013)

Grikke still runs the Ukrainian Management of Circus Training group. It is said that approximately 80 students are in the Circus. In recent years, students from the Grikke Circus have gained international recognition. They participated in the Budapest Circus Festival, where young Ukrainian performers showcased their skills, reflecting the resilience and dedication fostered within the Grikke Circus training programs.

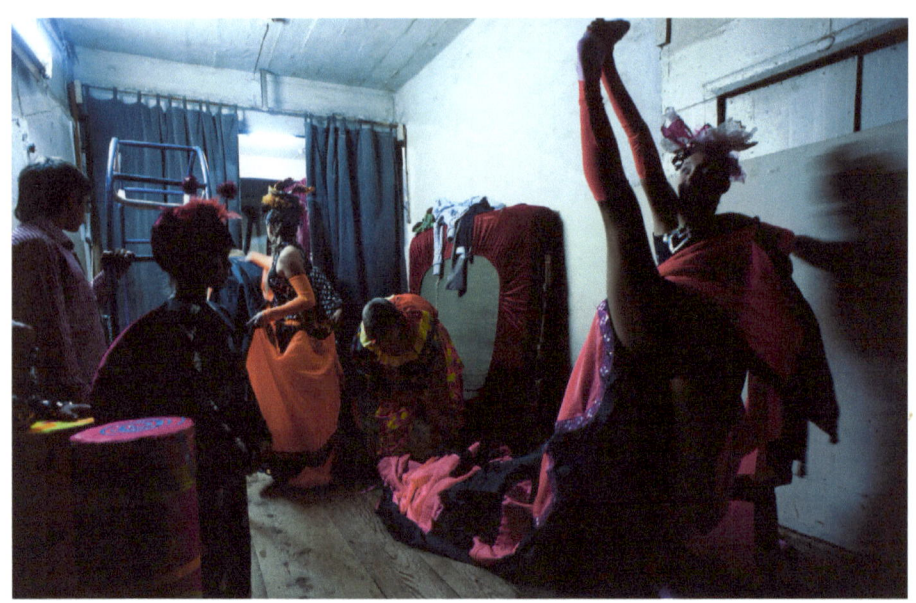

Images Mstyslav Chernov, a Ukrainian photojournalist, filmmaker, and war correspondent.

Students from Ukrainian circus schools, including those based in Kharkiv, have participated in circus festivals held in Budapest. In January 2023, young acrobats from various Ukrainian cities—such as Kharkiv, Kyiv, Dnipro, Odesa, and Donetsk - performed at the Yaskrava Arena Dnipra International Children's Circus Festival in Budapest, Hungary. These children, aged between 6 and 17, trained under challenging conditions, often in bomb shelters or without electricity due to the ongoing conflict in their home country.
https://bdnews24.com/lifestyle/zxhhtruxsw?utm_source=chatgpt.com

While specific details about the Grikke Circus building's students' participation are not mentioned, it's plausible that some performers from Kharkiv's circus community were involved, as the Kharkiv city's representation at the festival. Events like this have provided a platform for young Ukrainian circus artists to showcase their talents alongside their peers from Hungary, Switzerland, Mexico, and Italy, offering them a sense of normalcy and international recognition amid the hardships they face at home during the Russia invasion and continued bombing. *bdnews24.com*

The Budapest Circus Festival continues to be a significant venue for international circus talent, especially from Ukraine, celebrating the resilience and dedication of young performers worldwide.

Due to its limited capacity, a new circus building was constructed in Kharkiv in 1966 to accommodate larger audiences. While the Grikke building no longer hosts major performances, it continues to serve as a significant training center for aspiring circus artists in Ukraine. Whether it survives the destruction remains to be seen.

3.6. Kharkiv State Circus

As was previously noted, Kharkiv set up a temporary wooden circus designed by Prussian Wilhelm Sur in 1862. It was followed by Grikke in 1906.

The construction of the more permanent Grikke Circus by merchant Heinrich Grikke was constructed. This building still exists today and is still used for rehearsals and training purposes.

[openarium.ru+4scenic-circus.de+4Megan Starr Travel Blog+4Megan Starr Travel Blog](#)

The current circus building of the Kharkiv State Circus is the oldest in Ukraine. It was founded in 1886 and designed by architect V. A. Kasyan. The Circus opened its doors on April 9, 1974. A more modernist circus building it is typical of Soviet-era architecture. Its capacity is to accommodate over 2,000 spectators. It contains air conditioning which was unique and special elevators.

[Megan Starr Travel Blog+2Kathmandu](#)

3.7 Lviv State Circus

While men and women have been fighting at the front, their children have been exposed to the trauma of war with all its military and civilian authorities, loss and uncertainty.

The Lviv State Circus partnered with the Lviv Regional Military Administration and the Charity "My Dad Protects Ukraine,' to stage special performances for children across the region. The Lviv Military District Deputy Chief Khrystyna Zamulka said that 'Childhood should be happy. Unfortunately, our enemy is trying to take it away from Ukrainian children…'

A special performance was given as thanks to the defenders and parents fighting for Ukraine.

Children and their siblings with family were supported with travel into Lviv. The audience came from small towns and villages looking for small moments of joy in the devastation of bombings.

Kobzov, Circus in Ukraine © Mateusz Baj

Kobzov is like many travelling Ukrainian circuses. They were very traditional Soviet style circuses that would include animals performing with the artists.

The performers and the workers would travel together in caravans from town to town, during the better weather months of the year. Performers could be former sportsmen, people with disabilities or have come from regions affected by the destruction of their homes by the war with Russia. Performing or working for the circus was sometimes the only way to secure an income and support their internally displaced families.

The circuses using animals as performers were criticised for animal abuse, with conditions that were sometimes cruel and harmful. Finally, after years of lobbying by animals' activists, they eventually had to stop this practice when Ukraine's Ministry of Culture, Youth and Sports banned the use of animals from 2021. This had occurred earlier in Ukraine's Capital, Kyiv.

3.8 The Donetsk State Circus "Kosmos"

The historic Kosmos Circus building was completed in 1969. From the image you see a unique building shaped like a truncated cylinder. It is 60 meters wide and 30 meters high and unlike most traditional circus dome structures.

There is very little online information but that little available states that the Kosmos Circus has been a most historically significant center for circus arts in the region. The name Kosmos, Cosmos means 'space' in Russian. The Soviet-era fascination at the time was with space exploration. The circus was established in those Soviet times.

As of April 2025, the Donetsk State Circus 'Kosmos' managed to operate despite ongoing conflict in the region. Such institutions that are now in occupied Russian territory face disruptions in these conflict zones.

Although the Donetsk State Circus in Ukraine is classified as a major cultural institution, its situation is complicated due to the ongoing conflict. Scant information from 'ResearchGate' - a European networking site for researchers, noted, that while the circus itself still exists. This one and other Ukrainian circuses in the region are cut off from the rest of Ukraine. They are now under the control of the Russian-backed separatist government in the region.

As a further result of the hostilities in the Russian backed regions, Ukrainian circuses are facing financial loses by continuing to operate. Understandably, they have also lost talented artists to international circuses.

They are continuing performances to entertain and bring a sense of normal life to local communities in those zones. Such is the artistry and importance of circus in Ukraine, especially now from 2022- 2025.

So, let's remember the Donetsk State Circus 'Kosmos' or 'KOSMOZ' as holding a significant place in the cultural history of Donetsk and the broader Ukrainian Donbas region. It was part of a network of state-sponsored cultural institutions aimed at promoting performing arts across the USSR, in the day, and being especially popular among families and children.

3.9 Irpin State Circus

The Circus in Irpin, Ukraine has a unique and heartwarming presence, especially given Irpin's recent history. While Irpin is better known internationally now due to the tragic impact of the Russian invasion in 2022, before the war, it was a vibrant, green, suburban city near Kyiv known for its artistic community and cultural life - including local circuses and traveling troupes.

Irpin is the classical example of Ukrainian resistance. Russian forces entered the town and left an horrific trail of human and physical destruction but were prevented from pushing through and reaching the capital Kyiv. It was just 21 KM down the road.

After that insurgence of Irpin you would need an armed escort to drive through streets that were strewn with rubble, downed power lines and bodies still in the streets.

Terrifying stories emerged about the violence against civilians, of shootings and summary executions and of people being held by force in a basement. As the Ukrainian army regained control of the outskirts of Kyiv and were getting closer to Irpin, the

Russians retreated leaving Irpin destroyed with its inhabitants dead or gone. Very little life was left.

Ukrainians acted fast to clear rubble and vehicles littering the streets and the rebuild of Irpin began quickly. People returned, they needed to live and work. The city lives, there is business.

And so to circus life and performance in Irpin – it is alive and functioning. Here are some notable aspects about Irpin's Circus life:

- **Local Circus Troupes and Youth Programs:**

    Irpin has had local circus schools and performance programs for children and teens - part of Ukraine's broader cultural tradition of nurturing performing arts. These schools often combine acrobatics, dance, clowning, and gymnastics, training young people from an early age. The Irpin City House of Culture often hosted such performances and rehearsals.

- **Traveling Circuses:**

    Before the war, traveling circuses regularly stopped in Irpin, especially during the warmer months. These included classic Eastern European-style circuses with animal acts (though increasingly controversial), aerialists, jugglers, and clown performers. Pop- up circus tents and community fairs were common, especially for family outings.

- **Post-2022 Resilience and Revival:**

    After the destruction during the Battle of Irpin in early 2022, cultural and educational institutions, including performing arts schools and circus clubs, faced massive disruption. However, as Irpin has slowly rebuilt, cultural life — including circus arts — has shown signs of returning. There have been small performances and community- based shows designed to lift spirits and bring children joy in times of trauma. Kateryna Saksonova and Ivan Ventsyslavskyi managed to escape from the Russians and returned to begin teaching the children who were left or managed to return.

Some NGOs and international circus organizations (like Clowns Without Borders) have also visited Ukraine, including areas like Irpin, to offer therapeutic performances for children affected by war.

(Kuleba, 2024)

Ukrainian children in Irpin went through a lot of stress and had lost connection with basic events and people in their daily lives. The ones in Irpin witnessed their peers getting shot. Circus skills training was something that could pull them out of themselves and their severe situation for at least a few hours a day.

Kateryna and Ivan began trying to do something positive for these children because their situation was so incredibly tough. They taught the children to 'support each other, stick together, and share the experience – to make sure that no one is alone.' (Kuleba, 2024) Within the Ukrainian Circus Tradition with institutions like the Kyiv National Circus central to the cultural activities of the country, many Ukrainian circus artists toured internationally. Irpin, located close to Kyiv, benefited from this larger cultural 'ecosystem' of circus performers. While Irpin in Ukraine, does not have a formal 'state circus,' the city has a rich tradition of circus arts, particularly through its local studios and cultural institutions.

Compliment Circus Studio was stablished in 2008 by Kateryna Saksonova and Ivan Ventsyslavskyi. Both graduates of the Kyiv Academy of Circus and Variety Arts, the Compliment Circus Studio has been a cornerstone of Irpin's cultural scene. The studio was unique in that it focused on innovative performances blending choreography, acrobatics, and theatrical performance, and so they moved past traditional circus formats. (Kuleba, 2024)

During the Russian invasion in 2022, the studio's basement became a refuge for over 100 residents and the Ukrainian army. The studio and its equipment remained intact throughout the occupation.

The mats etc were dirty and messy from the soldiers but, when they handed it back it was with cleaned mats and chairs etc They just said these items belonged to the children. After Irpin's liberation, the studio resumed its activities, again symbolizing the city's resilience and commitment to cultural revival. (ui.org.ua+2Circus Life+2MASA Architects+2)

Built in 1954, the Irpin House of Culture served as a central hub for the city's artistic endeavours, hosting various creative studios, language clubs, and public events. The building featured an auditorium with nearly 500 seats and facilities for choreography, vocal, and drama classes. Unfortunately, it was significant damaged during the 2022 conflict. (ui.org.ua+1war.city+1)

Despite the enormous challenges, Irpin's dedication to the arts continues. Work is underway underway to restore its cultural landmarks and support institutions like the Compliment Circus Studio.(Kuleba, 2024)

3.10. Kryvyi Rih State Circus

The circus building in Kryvyi Rih stands as one of the few remaining examples of Soviet circus architecture in central Ukraine. It presented performances that combine traditional Ukrainian entertainment with international circus arts, featuring acrobats, clowns, and animal trainers.

It opened its doors on July 17, 1970, during a period of substantial cultural development in Soviet Ukraine. The circus venue organised regular performance schedules throughout the year. with shows running on weekends and special holiday programs during winter.

3.11 The DyvoCircus Festival

The image showing participants light up the ring with smartphone flashlights during a power outage during wartime in 2024 at DyvoCircus Festival at the Ukrainian National Circus (c)
CircusLife.com.ua

The DyvoCircus Festival is an international circus arts festival held in Kyiv, Ukraine. This festival is another major example of the resilience, strength and hope that Ukrainians demonstrate have despite the war in Ukraine.

During the 2024 threats of missile attacks, young circus artists performing in disciplines such as acrobats, juggling, clowning and aerial arts, continued defiantly with their performances.

During the event, a US based youth circus company, called Le PeTiT CiRqUe, presented the 'Award of Excellence' to outstanding young Ukrainian performers. Such was the respect by those international artists and companies attending and supporting circus in Ukraine.

Such international collaboration, provided the young Ukrainian artists opportunities to connect, learn, and grow in their craft with their peers. We can only imagine the feelings of respect that this would leave.

Generated with Ukraine's young artists.

CHAPTER 4

Ukraine's Cultural Ministry

So valuable is the importance of Circus and and entertainment medium that the Cultural Ministry of Ukraine has formerly recognised some TV channels, circuses and other cultural institutions as being 'critically important' companies during wartime. So important are they that some of the employees have by decree, been allowed to defer their military service. Dozens of media companies and TV channels have been deemed as critically important for the economy and livelihood of Ukrainians in this unique period of war.

The Directorate of Mobile Circus Teams, The State Circus Company, several circuses, theatres, operas and other such entities in Ukraine have been given this important 'critically important' status. (Interfax-Ukraine) This all with President Zelensky's newly approved laws to change the age of compulsory Military Service from 25 to 27. Such is the status of Circus in Ukraine.

4.1 Circus art is powerful in helping children during war

President Zelensky and the government of Ukraine have recognised that Circus arts have emerged as a powerful and innovative approach to trauma recovery, particularly for children and young people. By integrating physical movement, creative expression, and social interaction, circus-based skills developed as therapies, offer a holistic path to healing that is both engaging and empowering.

4.2 Circus Arts Supporting Trauma Recovery in Ukrainian Children

Circus arts can be a powerful tool in helping children build resilience during war by providing psychological, emotional, and physical benefits.

Resilience can be defined as 'the ability to maintain stable, healthy psychological and physical functioning despite being confronted with significant trauma'. (*Pacione et al. 2013*: 341)

There are five main areas of positive outcomes for children engaging in circus activities or training:

4.2.1. Emotional and Psychological Support

- Trauma Recovery: Circus activities - like acrobatics, juggling, and clowning offer a fun escape from the horrors of war. Such activity can help children process trauma in a safe, playful environment expending pent up energy.

- Boosts Confidence: Learning new tricks and performing them in front of others can give children a sense of achievement thus rebuilding their broken self-esteem.

- Encourages Expression: Circus skills, especially clowning and movement-based arts, allow children to express emotions non-verbally. This is common methodology and crucial for those struggling to articulate their trauma verbally.

4.2.2. Social Connection and Community Building

- Fosters a Sense of Belonging: War can disrupt social structures and family connections, but circus training creates a supportive community where children work together, trust each other, and develop friendships.

- Promotes Teamwork: Partner acrobatics and group performances require cooperation, fostering trust and social bonds even in displaced communities. If you are required to catch an acrobat it matters not whether you have a friend who has lost their life or limbs. Your circus partner needs you to concentrate and perform.

4.2.3. Physical and Mental Strength

- Encourages Body Awareness: Activities like balancing and tumbling help children regain a sense of control over their bodies. This can be especially important after experiencing violence or displacement or watching the same.

- Relieves Stress and Anxiety: Physical activity releases endorphins, reducing stress and anxiety levels common among children in war zones. Children naturally need to expend energy and no less in war time. Endorphins play a large part in human psychological wellbeing.

4.2.4. Creates a Sense of Normalcy and Joy

- Distraction from Conflict: Engaging in circus arts allows children to momentarily escape their reality and focus on something positive. Body and brain must connect to the exercise at hand.

- Instills Hope: Performing and having an audience applaud their efforts reinforces the idea that there is still joy and admiration in the world. Acceptance and reward of any kind is affirming.

4.2 5. Educational and Cognitive Development

- Improves Concentration and Problem-Solving: Learning circus tricks requires focus, perseverance, and creativity, all of which enhance cognitive resilience. Repetition increases the skill development and thus the positive reward and resilience.

- Encourages Adaptability: Circus teaches children how to fail safely, try again, and adapt, reinforcing resilience and perseverance. Falling is a child's common method of the struggle to learn a physical skill. Well used to develop circus skills.

CHAPTER 5

Organizations that have successfully used circus arts in war zones, refugee camps, and conflict-affected communities to support children's mental health and well- being.

There have been some key case studies and programs where circus arts have helped children build resilience in war-affected areas. Below are a selection. It is by no means complete:

5.1 Clowns Without Borders (CWB) – Global Impact in War Zones

Clowns Without Borders (CWB) is a nonprofit organization that brings laughter and relief to children in conflict zones. Their teams of clowns, jugglers, and circus performers travel to war-affected areas to provide performances and workshops. Clowns Without Borders International (CWBI) is a non-operational umbrella organization that supports and connects 13 Clowns Without Borders countries worldwide. CWBI's works to organise communication and cooperation between these chapters/countries. They have delivered performances to Ukraine.

Children that are found in refugee camps often suffer from PTSD, anxiety, and depression due to war and displacement.

CWB conducts performances and interactive workshops in many refugee camps, wherever safe to do so. They create spaces for children to experience joy and laughter.

https://clownswithoutborders.org/ukrainian-refugees-co-create/

It is found that even brief moments of play helped children release fear and anxiety, allowing them to engage more positively with caregivers and peers.

Over time, children showed increased participation, self-confidence, and a willingness to express themselves.

Quote from a field report:
'A mother from Lviv told us, This is the first time in months I've seen my child smile.'

https://www.theflyingseagullproject.com/

5.2 The Flying Seagull Project – Performing in Conflict Zones

This UK-based charity brings circus skills, magic, and games to children in war-torn and refugee settings.

'When play becomes a luxury, a child's world shrinks into the daily struggles of premature adulthood.' The Flying Seagul Project uses clowning, magic, games and arts workshops to replace fear and uncertainty. This is always with positive human connections based on respect, happiness and laughter.

The Flying Seagull Project runs interactive clowning workshops, juggling sessions, and music performances in displacement camps of countries where there is conflict.

It is commonly noticed that children are initially hesitant to participate but eventually lose their fear and inhibitions and begin engaging, laughing, and rediscovering play.

Long-term Benefits:

- Increased social interaction and trust-building among children.
- Improvements in emotional expression, reducing aggressive or withdrawn behaviors.
- Parents reported that their children slept better and had fewer nightmares after circus sessions.

Founder's insight: 'Laughter is a universal language that helps children heal. If we can make them giggle, we give them back their childhood for a moment.' https://www.theflyingseagullproject.com/

5.3 Zip Zap Circus – South Africa's Work with Child Soldiers & Refugees

Originally based in South Africa, Zip Zap Circus has expanded its outreach to war-affected children in Africa.

Zip Zap was born in 1992 from a simple dream, a trapeze bar in a tree, a costume box and a rusty car. It was established by South African born Brent van Rensburg and his French wife, Laurence Estève with a dream to use the circus as a tool to bridge socio-economic gaps. They wanted to inspire and empower young people to build a new culture of peaceful co-existence in South Africa. They were inspired by the late Nelson Mandela.

In the Democratic Republic of Congo where children were forcibly recruited into armed groups, they were found to be suffering from severe trauma and had difficulty reintegrating into society.

Zip Zap became involved and introduced circus training (acrobatics, juggling, clowning) as a form of psychosocial

https://www.zip-zap.org/

rehabilitation. It was found, that learning circus skills, gave children a positive identity beyond being former soldiers.

Interestingly many children transitioned into circus trainers themselves, thus creating a cycle of mentorship and empowerment. The children who engaged in circus arts showed higher rates of successful reintegration into schools and communities compared to those who only received traditional therapy.

Emotional relief from such programmes sees the development of laughter and play reducing stress and anxiety in war-affected children.

Social bonding from Circus programmes fosters teamwork and social trust, crucial for displaced or traumatized children.

Psychosocial healing, developing from non-verbal expression through circus arts, helps children process trauma in a non-threatening way.

There is a feeling of hope and empowerment. achieved by learning new skills. Children's confidence is restored, and they achieve a sense of control over their lives.

5.4 Cirque Hors Piste (Canada)

The programme for social circus and trauma, uses circus to support trauma recovery, emotional regulation and mind-body reconnection. It includes children affected by homelessness and displacement. (Cirque Hors Piste, 2018)

https://www.zip-zap.org/

https://cirquehorspiste.com

CHAPTER 6

Resilience, Cultural and Emotional power of Circus in Ukraine

Earlier you read that some Ukrainian circus schools and companies have remained active during the Russian invasion of Ukraine. They are showing great resilience by adapting to the challenges of blackouts, air raids, and displacement.

Some shows have continued, serving as morale-boosting events for children and families. The arts have done what the arts have done for decades, entertaining and bringing joy and artistry to people as a distraction in war time.

The Circus is very much part of that artistry in action. Thanks to the President's decree to continue such entertainment for Ukrainians, deeming it very important for their psychological health.

The circus is being used not just for entertainment, but as a form of psychological relief and cultural resistance, especially for displaced children. There are many internally displaced Ukrainian children being taken care of by people and agencies.

Circus as a form of cultural resistance during war is a fascinating phenomenon. In past times of conflict or war, circus performers and companies have used their art to uplift morale, preserve cultural identity and even challenge oppression.

6.1. Soviet and Eastern European Resistance and Circus

During WWII, Soviet circus artists were mobilized to entertain troops and citizens, keeping spirits high while subtly embedding messages of defiance against Nazi occupation. In Eastern Europe under Soviet rule, circus performances often carried hidden critiques of authoritarian regimes. This was through satire, absurdity, and symbolic acts. Their audience at whom this was directed was often totally oblivious.

6.1 Ukraine's Circus in the War Against Russia

The circus is more than alive in Ukraine. It's saving lives, one laugh, one backflip, one balancing act and smile at a time.

Since Russia's full-scale invasion of Ukraine in 2022, Ukrainian circus artists have performed in bomb shelters, refugee centres, and front-line areas, using acrobatics and clowning to bring hope amid destruction. In many cases risking their very own lives to entertain. In the daily video feeds from army battalions on social media, we witness soldiers, both men and women, performing tricks for their fellow soldiers during times of respite. Backflips, cartwheels, balancing acts and juggling are common skill sets.

Performers have taken their acts abroad to raise awareness and funds for humanitarian efforts, using circus as a tool of soft resistance.

Circus acts, by their very nature, embody resilience especially in times of trouble, often defying gravity and limits and equally mirroring the fight for survival and cultural endurance. Through an artform, the artform of circus.

CHAPTER 7

Circus as Resistance to Oppression

This is a most fascinating notion.

- Circus defies gravity and oppression/restraints. Acrobatics and feats of circus skills symbolize human endurance and resilience. People love to witness such feats and watch with awe and apprehension the feats of athleticism and strength, often questioning whether they would be capable of performing the same or, wondering how it is possible to humanly achieve such acts? Each time we witness a high wired circus act we watch with trepidation hoping the performer will succeed.

- Circus speaks no verbal language - Visual storytelling allows compelling communication even in occupied or censored environments. Soldiers on a battlefield striving to entertain nervous or exhausted fighters with intrepid acrobatics. Children who are nonverbal are seen attempting circus skills with balls or doing floor rolls as therapy. Through the example of circus, perhaps we can all start looking at ourselves and each other in terms of success rather than failure. Circus skills give autistic children the opportunity to achieve physical feats that they may have been told are impossible for them to attain, promoting new levels of self-confidence and new levels of connection between the children and their families. (Seymour, 2012)

Seymour in her Master's thesis states, that the environment of creative chaos developed in circus is particularly beneficial for children with autism; that the practice and philosophy of circus values both difference and inclusivity, helping to build community; that philosophy and cultural theory can provide insights into how circus 'works' for autistic children and their families; and that participation in circus can change how people understand the world and each other. (Seymour, 2012)

- Circus brings People Together – Collective joy and shared spectacles during performances brings collective joy and a sharing of the experience. Circus builds unity against oppression.

- Circus challenges Authoritarianism – Satire, clowning, and physical humour provide subtle but powerful social commentary. As demonstrated on Facebook and other social media regarding political or organisational events.

Seymour sees the circus is a culture where difference is not only embraced, but also celebrated; a place where 'freaks', social misfits and oddities in general have found a way to belong and thrive, especially since the 1800s. Circus has a history steeped in the concept of being different and unorthodox. It encourages that rules and expectations about physical abilities be bent and broken in order to create a dynamic space that changes the way we see and experience the human form and reorganises our ideas of what bodies are capable of doing. The lights shining upon an aerialist as she flies defying gravity; the sound of the drum roll as acrobats balance delicately upon each others' shoulders, keeping the audience in suspense as to what might happen if they slip or fall.

Seymour uses the term 'autistic spectrum' as this is the most commonly accepted medical term, however this, and the term 'special needs' are both labels that are capable of locking children into categories and 'boxes', which we try to avoid when working with children and circus. She states, 'Circus performers amaze onlookers, but equally they can amaze performers. Social circus allows children to amaze themselves. This project explores how amazing yourself can be especially important for children too often seen as problems, who can come to see themselves that way too.' (Seymour, 2012. pp 6,7)

CHAPTER 8

Trauma Recovery and Circus Arts Therapy

Clearly circus arts have emerged as a powerful and innovative response to trauma recovery, particularly for children and young people. By integrating physical movement, creative expression, and social interaction, circus-based therapies offer a holistic path to healing that is both engaging and empowering.

Nowadays, many organizations and therapists are recognizing the potential of circus arts therapy and incorporating it into their programs. From children with developmental disorders to adults recovering from trauma or addiction, circus arts provide a non-traditional avenue for healing and rehabilitation. The combination of physical exercise, emotional expression, and social engagement makes circus arts a unique and holistic form of therapy. There are many organisations worldwide that are incorporating circus arts into therapies for children and adults.

CIRCUS ARTS INSTITUTE https://www.circusartsinstitute.com/Circus-Arts-Therapy.html?utm_source=chatgpt.com

Programmes that are given different names but revolve around trauma treatment with children and adults, especially those who are struggling with issues in their life they are stressed about or feel they are insurmountable. These programmes specialize in trauma, anxiety, and neurodivergence for all people usually 3 years old and up. It is often labelled 'play therapy.'

More importantly the treatment is referred to as 'trauma-informed play therapy', combining principles of trauma-informed care with the foundational methods of play therapy. Trauma-informed care recognizes the presence of trauma and its deep and underlying effects, but it depends an environment where safety, trust, and self-control are first and foremost. Play therapy provides children with a way to communicate through toys, games, and creative activities, thus bypassing language limitations. It offers a natural outlet for emotions.

https://www.purpleskycounseling.com/blog/mckenzie-bradford-lcsw-trauma-informed-play- therapy-for-children?utm_source=chatgpt.com

Circus arts therapy offers a non-threatening space where participants can explore their abilities without fear of judgment. This playful setting encourages individuals to take risks, make mistakes, and learn from them, fostering resilience and adaptability. Many circus activities are group-based, promoting teamwork, communication, and trust among participants. This collaborative aspect can help individuals rebuild social connections and reduce feelings of isolation often associated with trauma. It is certainly true with children at circus schools in Ukraine.

In Australia, initiatives like the Cirkidz program in Adelaide have demonstrated the mental health benefits of circus arts for children. Research from the University of South Australia indicates that for every dollar invested in children's circus programs, there is a social return of seven dollars, highlighting the cost-effectiveness of such interventions.

Cirkids

https://www.google.com/url?sa=t&source=web&rct=j&opi=89978449&url=https://www.cirkidz. org.au/&ved=2ahUKEwjVhov_pISNAxUUR2cHHUVbB8YQFnoECDcQAQ&usg=AOvVaw3XSDru4 o406vRHK95hTFo0

https://www.unisa.edu.au/unisanews/2019/may/story2/?utm_source=chatgpt.com

The SA Circus Centre and UniSA are dedicated to the ongoing research into Why Circus Works.

Circus in Schools 2015: Research Summary Key Findings:

Statistically significant increase of troupe student's means scores for Planning and Task Management compared to their peers (i.e. the non-troupe, control group students)

Statistically significant difference between the beneficial decrease in one negative motivation and engagement to learning factor (Disengagement) for students involved in the Cirkidz troupe compared to their peers.

These findings indicate that involvement by students in the regular circus-based skills training directly affected their levels of motivation and engagement to learning.

UniSA's Dr Richard McGrath's research with Cirkidz about children participating in circus skills training and how this can improve their mental health tells us that for every $1 invested, $7 of savings is generated via improvements in children's health and wellbeing due to participation in our circus programs.

Globally, organizations like CircusAid utilize circus arts to support communities affected by trauma, offering workshops and performances that foster healing and resilience.

www.circusaid.com

CircusAid promotes positive social and emotional health for political and environmental refugees by creating opportunities for problem solving, teamwork, increased self- confidence and most of all, joy and laughter through engagement in circus activities during the resettlement process. www.circusaid.com

8.1 What Makes a Circus 'Trauma-Informed?'

This question is one that encompasses so much. People who plan 'trauma-informed circus must examine every part of the programme to build skills teaching around the needs of children or people who have experienced trauma. Deciding what skills will be taught and how they will be taught, based upon the ages and situation of the participants.

Trauma -informed circus training or teaching relies upon teachers and support staff who have an understanding, possibly first hand understanding of the trauma faced by the participants. As in Ukraine. At times, where possible, or, as in the case of Ukrainian children who have lost a parent or both parents, there needs to be someone accompanying, who is their carer or a family member. The classes are built around the needs of the children or people who have experienced trauma.

The list of reference material at the end of this book notes some specific considerations in teaching such circus art. They are briefly outlined under specific headings and, are in fact the general considerations in teaching circus art. They synthesise the information already outlined albeit more simply:

1. **Safety First - Physical *and* Emotional**
   - Instructors are trained, or encouraged, to create a calm, predictable, and non- judgmental environment.
   - Activities are carefully structured to avoid overwhelming or triggering the nervous system.
   - Consent and choice are emphasized: kids are never forced to perform or tackle a skill until they feel confident.

2. **Body Awareness and Regulation**
   - Many trauma-informed circus programs use gentle movement (like balance, juggling, or aerial silk) to help participants reconnect with their bodies in a safe, empowering way.
   - These activities improve nervous system regulation, which can help with anxiety, focus, and emotional control.

3. **Rebuilding Trust and Connection**
   - Team-based circus acts like partner acrobatics, clowning, or group juggling encourage safe social interaction and cooperation.
   - These experiences help rebuild a sense of trust in others - something often damaged by trauma.

4. **Empowerment Through Mastery**
   - Learning circus skills (even small ones!) helps kids feel a sense of control, progress, and success.
   - Trauma often makes people feel powerless. In circus, every small win - catching a ball, standing on a tightrope, or making someone laugh - is an act of reclaiming strength.

5. **Expression Without Words**
   - For children who have experienced war, displacement, or loss, it can be hard - or impossible- to talk about their feelings.
   - Circus allows for creative, nonverbal expression through movement, performance, and play.
   - Clowning, for example, can help kids process sadness or fear through exaggerated, symbolic gestures.

8.2. Who Designs Trauma-Informed Circus Programs?

They are often co-developed by:

- Circus educators
- Psychologists or trauma therapists
- Social workers
- Community arts organizations

One example is Cirque du Monde (an outreach arm of Cirque du Soleil), which runs trauma-informed programs for at-risk youth worldwide. In Ukraine and refugee communities, smaller circus groups are adapting similar methods for war-affected children.

Trauma-informed circus is not therapy *instead* of counselling - but it *is* and can be deeply therapeutic, combining all elements of the joy and playfulness of circus, the stability and focus of skill building and the healing power of human connection.

Something our traumatised Ukrainian children desperately need.

8.3 Occupational deprivation

Proponents of CircusAid, talk about occupational deprivation. 'This is a situation when 'someone is deprived of participating in activities that give them meaning. It can lead to depression and anxiety, which can lead to mental illness. Without social and occupational support, thousands of people will develop mental health issues. Addressing occupational health in refugee camps and support centres is not just about supporting refugees, but also about protecting the communities already in existence.' *https://www.circusaid.com/*

This definition enhances what we understand about trauma. When we think about trauma and children experiencing trauma, we can see that the regular, normal, often trivial daily activities and routines that make up a child's world, no matter how meaningless, can be totally disrupted. 'This basic human need becomes challenging during resettlement where there are heavy restrictions on choice, opportunity, accessibility, freedom, and resources.' *https://www.circusaid.com/*

There are many such examples around the world such as Lombok's 'Train the Trainer' Project through CircusAid. Their project provided 847 free CircusAid experiences to local communities in Lombok, Indonesia to introduce occupational therapy practices. It had a wider impact as it unified health and education professionals in service delivery for environmental refugees, at-risk youth, and women survivors of sexual assault.

https://www.cirusaid.com/lombok

CHAPTER 9

Circus Schools and Academies

Interested people and supporters of such circus skills and therapies often wish to know the best circus training programmes in the world. There are too many to list and detail, but a few crucial ones are included for further information and exploration.

Each country has organisations, schools and academies. Not all are accredited, and parents should check before signing up their children into their classes. Always ensure children or adults enrolled are working with professionals. Some schools teach some semblance of simple skills in children's daily learning programmes. Usually with the physical education professional attached to the school.

Ukraine

Kyiv Municipal Academy of Circus and variety Arts continues to train world-class acrobats, clowns, jugglers and aerialists. Many Ukrainian Circus Academies have a long and respected tradition of circus arts, dating back to the Soviet era. All of the circus schools outlined in this publication have maintained a high rigour and trained some memorable circus athletes.

https://kmaecm.edu.ua/en/home-english
(this video is fantastic to view!)

https://circuscenter.org/

https://sancaseattle.org/

USA

It is said that the San Francisco's Circus Center is probably the best professional training program in the USA. *https://circuscenter.org/*

Seattle's School of New Circus Arts (SANCA) SANCA is noted as one of the nation's largest and highly regarded circus schools in the US, both by number of students and square footage.

New England Center for Circus Arts (NECCA) is also very highly regarded.

https://necenterforcircusarts.org/

Many such centres are nonprofit. They are committed to the people who join their programmes and the community within which they operate. They often rely fully on generous donors to offer a centre that is accessible to everyone. Sometimes they may receive financial assistance from a local government authority. They are places where creativity and artistry soar, and where the seemingly impossible becomes possible- every single day.

Australia

The National Institute of Circus Arts, based in Melbourne, Victoria, is the premier institute to offer a degree course in Circus Arts. They have programs for ages 5-80 years. NICA is a government-accredited tertiary-level circus school in Australia. It is located in the suburb of Prahran, Victoria.

NICA is also a national not-for-profit arts training institute and a registered cultural organisation. It is primarily funded by the Australian Government through the Department of Communications and the Arts. It is one of eight elite arts training organisations comprising the Arts8, and members of the Federation of European Circus Schools (FEDEC). They provide a resource that can be accessed however, please read the information below:

https://www.clearinghouseforsport.gov.au/data/assets/pdf_file/0005/864383/33 297_CompBk_Circus_final_ART.pdf

Acknowledgments

The Australian Sports Commission wishes to acknowledge the contribution of the following people and organisations to the production of this resource.

Activities included within the Circus Companion Book have been adapted from the Playing for Life Resource Kit, with the assistance of Kathryn Montgomery (Community Circus Trainer – National Institute of Circus Arts), Andrea Ousley (Community Circus Trainer – National Institute of Circus Arts) and Meredith Kelly (AASC). These contributors also provided significant input for the inclusion of new activities and the circus-specific content.

Gayle Rogers (ACHPER/Schools Network), Sue Cormack (ACHPER/Schools Network), Bruce Knights (Keilor Downs Secondary College) and Les Bee developed the content for the introduction and principles for how and when to change activities.

The editorial team of Creating Excellence Consulting, Wenda Donaldson (AASC), Teena Jackson (AASC), Lainie Houston (AASC), Melissa Backhouse (Junior Sport Unit) and Ashley Beaver (AASC) developed, proofread and edited written materials and significantly contributed to the overall content and format of the final product.

Disclaimer

The Playing for Life companion books have been designed for use with students aged 4–12. Each book assumes that each student is healthy and has no medical condition, disability, illness, impairment or other reason that may impact, limit or restrict their involvement in sport or other physical activity. A student should not be allowed to participate in an activity if any medical, physical or other factor indicates that they are not suited to that activity. Where there are any queries or concerns about such matters, the consent of the student's parent or guardian should be obtained before allowing participation. While care has been taken in the preparation of these books, the publisher and authors do not accept any liability arising from the use of the books including, without limitation, from any activities described in the books. © Australian sports commission 2007

Their work is copyright. I have included the link for your information. Apart from any fair dealing for the purpose of private study, research, criticism or review as permitted under the Copyright Act 1968 and subsequent amendments, no part of their publication may be reproduced, stored in a retrieval system, or transmitted in any form or by any means, electronic, mechanical, photocopying, recording or otherwise, without prior written permission from the Australian Sports Commission. Requests and enquiries concerning reproduction should be addressed to the copyright officer (email: copyright@ausport.gov.au).

CHAPTER 10

International Support & Touring Programs

Ukrainian circus artists have been touring Europe and beyond, raising funds for humanitarian aid. Some foreign circus groups have invited Ukrainian children to participate in training camps and residencies, offering them a temporary respite and new opportunities.

Poland, Germany, France and Lithuania's international circus schools and companies have opened their doors to displaced Ukrainian children. For example, the Zirkus Zaretti in Germany holds camps; the Ecole Nationale de Cirque de Chatellerault has allowed Ukrainian refugee children to join their youth programmes and, the Social Circus School in Lithuania has developed a special trauma-based programme linking circus with therapy for war traumatised children from Ukraine.

The performers, La Putyka, in a photo by Lukáš Bíba

La Putyka builds bridges across language barriers in a stirring and thought-provoking circus act. The experience of a group of Czech and Ukrainian performers was brought together by a devastating conflict. The Ukrainian and Czech performers did not have a common language to communicate with and so they used a mix of English, Czech and Russian. The Ukrainian performers were instrumental in one scene where they portrayed the tradition of welcoming guests with bread and salt. This is such a traditional ceremony that has been used for centuries to welcome people to a Ukrainian gathering.

More information about La Putyka can be found online
https://www.laputyka.cz/en/company

The Director of La Putyka created a few shows that were performed in Prague but also at the Edinburgh Festival Fringe, followed by 43 shows in 24 days. (Caloianu, 2022)

The performers, La Putyka, in a photo by Lukáš Bíba

Students arrived at Budapest from Kyiv Academy of Circus and Variety Arts and Kharkiv Circus Schools

https://stagelync.com/news/the-circus-world-has-united-for-ukraine

Some other organisations involved in rescue efforts of Ukrainian circus performers:

This wonderful attitude has linked these countries through circus initiatives for war traumatised Ukrainian children.

Many organisations and circus schools have been involved in rescue attempts of Ukrainian students. Honis in 2022 listed them, but they and not limited to:

- Young Stage Festival, Switzerland
- Capital Circus of Budapest
- Baltijas Cirks – Latvia
- Circus Belly – Austria
- Rosante group – Italy
- Cirque Alexandre Bouglione
- Circus Olympia – Germany
- Cirkus Syd – Sweden
- Circus Brazil Jack
- Fondazione Cirko Vertigo
- Centre International des Arts en Mouvement (CIAM) – International Center for Arts in Motion
- Cheval Art Action LA Maison de Nina
- Balance Akrobatika & Torna Club Wanjanini

- Inspirál circus center Circus Studio Folie
- Recirquel Company CIRCO RICHMOON
- Circus-Luna-Hof
- National Circus Art Center CircO Hannover CircArtive School
- Zirkusschule Dobbelino Ines Rosemann
- Circus Schatzinsel (Vuesch gGmbH) Hakasirkus
- Jugendkulturarbeit e.V.; Educational institution "Internationale Jugendprojektehaus (IJP)" in Oldenburg
- Jokes die Circusschule e.V. Die Zirkusfabrik
- Circus CabuwAzi Treptow Circus Waldoni
- Cirkus Gymnasiet/ Cirkus Cirkör Rambazotti
- Zirkus Trainingszentrum Fly Norrköpings ungdomscirkus
- The Oak Circus Centre Circus Flora Circusjuventas
- Le PeTiT CiRqUe Satasirkus ry Cnac
- Kristian Kristof Natalia Demjen Rikardo Ledman Gabor Karsa
- Cirko Sapiens
- Circus Works Devoran Escola Circo VagaMundo Oulun Tähtisirkus
- LATIBUL Theater- und Zirkuspädagogisches Zentrum Köln Sirkuskoulu Rainbow
- EPA
- Pukinmäki Art Schools, Pukinmäki Circus School Zirkus Tasifan
- Kinder- und Jugendzirkus Paletti e.V. CIRCUS BOSCH/La Scuola di Circo Circus Rotjeknor
- Freie Waldorfschule Wetterau

- INAC INSTITUTO NACIONAL DE ARTES DO CIRCO
- Circus und Zeltpunkt Montelino Cirque Intense Preparatory School Cirka Cirkus
- Merscheider Turnverein Circus Odyssey – Lithuania Palazzo – Germany
- The Circus Community in Lublin – Poland Circo Peppino Medini – Italy
- Nouveau Cirque Zavatta – France Circus studio folie, Tallinn – Estonia
- Culpepper and Merriweather circus – USA Hudson's circus – Australia
- Västerås, Sweden
- United Kingdom ~ Let's Circus Gycklargruppen TRiX
- The wonder circus Circus Barlay
- Mirene Cardinali Circus
- Cork La Putyka – Czech Republic Recirquel – Hungary
- Sky crew circus arts – Greece (Honis, 2022)

10.2 How Ukraine's internally displaced children are finding hope during war time within Ukraine

Organizations like Clowns Without Borders and Ukraine's own Dzyga Circus have sent and deployed teams of performers into shelters, hospitals. and conflict zones of IDP (internally displaced persons) camps.

In Kharkiv, where schools were bombed and playgrounds destroyed very early in the invasion by Russia, clowns have turned underground shelters into stages. Sometimes children laugh, for the first time in days or weeks, breaking through the fog of fear and sadness.

As we know and psychologists confirm that laughter releases endorphins, lowers stress hormones, and helps children reconnect with a sense of safety, even if temporarily.

'When I see my son laugh at the clowns, it's like he remembers he's still a child,' said one mother in a Lviv shelter. 'For five minutes, he forgets the war.'

The gift of laughter brings a moment of joy that that is part of a child's innate need for play.

As noted, the Circus organisations within Ukraine are all attempting to run programmes with the complete support of Ukraine's President and his cultural and entertainment organisational leadership.

Even as the war continues, Ukrainian circus artists - young and old - are keeping their national identity alive through performance.

- Traditional Ukrainian motifs are woven into costumes and stories.
- Shows on tour across Europe often highlight themes of resilience, displacement, and hope.

Some Ukrainian children have begun telling their stories through clowning or acrobatic theatre, through circus art. They have found a way of reclaiming their narrative, of telling their story, in a way that words alone cannot. They are saying, 'I am Ukrainian. I am not a

Nazi, I am not a Russian, I am not someone who wants to hurt you or your family, I love my country, and I love who I am.'

Circus performers are using traditional Ukrainian motifs interwoven or stitched into their costumes and circus stories.

When travelling or included in circus companies, Ukrainian performers are making it quite clear where they have come from by the training clothes they wear, or flags draped around them and the companies employing them are enabling this.

Some Ukrainian artists have relocated and brought Ukrainian circus talent to international stages, often utilising performances to raise awareness and support for Ukraine.

This national pride has transcended sporting arenas as well as other entertainment theatres and circus events where Ukrainians are performing.

Many Ukrainian performers have, in the past, and still do tour with top global companies such as *Cirque de Soleil, Circus Roncalli* and *Cirque Eloize*.

10.3. The Circus as Cultural Resistance

Circus as a form of cultural resistance during war is a fascinating phenomenon.

Ward stated that 'circus can be magical and entertaining but it can also be subversive and political.' (Ward, 2019)

This is not new, and historically we have seen troops visit war zones to lift morale, preserve cultural identity and sometimes challenge oppression. In the video and photographic feeds that have emerged from the Ukrainian Armed Forces have shown all the facets of entertainment, morale boosting and challenging the oppressor.

Circus as an art form has constantly adapted and re-invented itself to meet the needs of a changing society. During WWII, Soviet circus artists did this while embedding messages of defiance into their performances against the Nazi occupier. In opposition under Soviet rule, circus was criticising authoritarian regimes through circus satire and unique acts. Clowns were able to subtly criticise the regime with humour.

CHAPTER 11

Overseas Circus Companies with Ukrainian Performers

11.1 Cirque du Soleil

Most people would have been fortunate to have attended a performance of Cirque de Soleil over the years. If you were as interested in the performers as I have always been, you would have checked their place of origin I the programme booklet. Ukraine has always had circus artists in the Cirque troops over the years.

The Cirque du Soleil phenomenon started in Baie-Saint-Paul, a small town near Québec City in Canada. There, in the early eighties, a group of colourful characters roamed the streets, striding/walking on stilts, juggling, dancing, breathing fire, and playing music.

They were Les Échassiers (a French wader bird with long legs) de Baie-Saint-Paul (the Baie-Saint-Paul Stilt walkers). This was a street theatre group founded by Gilles Ste- Croix, a Canadian entrepreneur and the vice president and co-creator of Cirque du Soleil. Already, the townsfolk were impressed and intrigued by the young performers – including Guy Laliberté who co-founded Cirque du Soleil.

People everywhere have been amazed at the skills of the acrobats and circus performers who tour with this elite global company, Cirque du Soleil, the largest contemporary circus in the world.

The company base is located in the inner-city area of Saint-Michel, Montreal. Guy Laliberté OC (Officer of the Order of Canada) CQ (Companion of the Order of Quebec), a highly honoured Canadian billionaire businessman, poker player and Gilles Ste-Croix. co-founded Cirque du Soleil in June 1984. They have employed some of the finest Ukrainian circus performers since then.

Cirque du Soleil was originally set up with the assistance of the Quebec government and developed as part of the celebrations surrounding the 450th anniversary of Jacques Cartier's arrival in Canada. The first production, Le Grand Tour debut in the small Quebec town of Gaspé, was then performed in 10 other cities throughout the province. Cirque du Soleil Entertainment Group is a world leader in live entertainment.

For more information about Cirque du Soleil Entertainment Group, please visit *cirquedusoleil.com*. I have included some interesting pieces of general information. The headquarters are set up with every type of apparatus and training facility to develop the extraordinary athletes. Athletes, acrobats and every iteration of performer, are administered to as if they are Olympic athletes. All health, psychological and medical requirements are completely considered throughout all training programmes.

Once you are employed for a place with a Cirque du Soleil show, where programmes change from time to time, performers attend the Studio for a few weeks or months of preliminary training before joining a show. The artists undergo artistic and acrobatic training while at the Creation Studio. Artists can be artistic and acrobatic gymnastics, tumbling, acrosport, swimming, diving, dance, singing, music and, especially, circus arts. Cirque du Soleil artists hail from some fifty nationalities.

Around one hundred trainers from around the world supervise performer training programs. There are specialists in dance, theatre, singing, and acrobatics in addition to these coaches and trainers. Each artist is taken care of by an interdisciplinary team of highly qualified specialists. They are employed to ensuring the physical and psychological well-being of each artist by ensuring a controlled and safe environment for optimal performance skill outcome.

https://www.cirquedusoleil.com/

https://www.cirquedusoleil.com/

There is usually a 7-piece band that includes a bandleader/drummer, bass and double bass player, percussionist, violinist, wind instruments player, keyboard player, guitarist, plus one singer, and in almost all of Cirque du Soleil shows, the music is performed live. Unlike your classical musical, the Cirque music needs to adapt and coordinate with what is going on stage. So much so that the band leader, the musicians, the singers and the sound staff are in constant communication through the use of highly sophisticated unobtrusive headsets and microphones. The audience has no notion of such technical support to ensure a seamless transition of acts throughout the performance.

The musical score for OVO based upon the insect world, was composed by Berna Ceppas, an independent, Brazilian, original music composer, music, actor, music producer, and sound director. He combined the sounds of bossa nova and samba with funk and electro music. As a Brazilian musician included a lot of percussion in the score.

Cirque de Soleil sets and technicalities are of such high quality which I, as an amateur music critic, can attest to, having attended each Cirque show shown in Perth Western Australia. The one show seen overseas was 'O', at the Bellagio Hotel & Casino, in Las Vegas. That was some years ago and it left me 'gobsmacked.'

O was an outstanding production with a water stage rising and falling. The action led to riveting, mesmerising vision and, me completely marvelling at the technical expertise and performance of the Cirque de Soleil company in that show.

https://www.cirquedusoleil.com/press/kits/corporate/about-cirque

11.2. Circus Roncalli

The German *Circus Roncalli*, founded by Bernhard Paul and Andre Heller in 1976 and *Cirque Éloize*, in Montreal Quebec, are a lesser-known circus entertainment  companies to Australians. Both Companies have continually attracted Ukrainian circus talent.

Circus Roncalli is a German professional circus founded in 1976 by Bernhard Paul and André Heller. Austrian circus director, clown and director Bernhard together with André Heller founded the Circus Roncalli and the Wintergarten Varieté in Berlin. Bernhard envisaged a different, special circus. He was instrumental in developing the world of the ring. The name of the company was suggested by fellow Austrian Peter Hajek and his film script writer Sarah Roncalli, Tochter des Mondes [Sarah Roncalli, Daughter of the Moon]. This was named after Pope John XXIII· Whose lay name was, Angelo Giuseppe Roncalli and the founders were inspired by his reform agenda of the church. They also like the sound of it.

During the Russian war with Ukraine, some artists relocated and continue to bring Ukrainian circus talent to international stages, often utilizing performances to raise essential awareness and support for Ukraine. Ukrainian athletes training out of the country continued to train and compete in international meets also raising awareness for Ukraine. Thay are champions, spurred on to shine a light on their countrymen and women fighting for democracy and peace.

11.3 The Jewish Circus Resistance in Nazi Germany

Jewish circus families, like the Lorch family in Germany, used their performances to survive and, in some cases, help others escape persecution.

The Lorch Circus was large, successful and famous throughout Europe until antisemitism in Germany forced the Lorch Circus out of business. The family joined the Althoff Circus, to make a living, but also attempting to stay alive. Adolf Althoff saved them and stated, 'We circus people see no difference between races or religions. Circus people live in the entire world and are of the entire world.'

The Lorch Family Circus in 1932
(courtesy of Staatliche Museen zu Berlin)

Irene Danner-Storm's maternal family, The Lorch family, was one of a few Jewish families who ran their own circuses in Germany for generations before the rise of the National Socialists. The Lorch Circus was large, successful and famous throughout all of Europe. Their family's Risley act travelled as far as the United States and

South America. Everything changed when -growing antisemitism in Germany forced the Lorch Circus out of business and soon, with the Nazi's rise to power, Jews were sent to ghettos and camps. The Lorchs' very lives were in danger. Joining the Althoff Circus was not only a means to make a living, it was a desperate attempt to stay alive.

As the war progressed, the Althoff Circus travelled all over Germany and Austria with Irene performing on its sawdust stage. In 1942, after a few of her family members were deported to Auschwitz, Irene and Peter persuaded Adolf and Maria Althoff to extend their generosity to Irene's mother, father and sister, who were allowed to join them at the circus.

When SS officers showed up for surprise inspections, Adolf cleverly distracted them with his amusing tales and an abundance of alcohol, while Mohammed helped the family hide. Althoff's protection saved their lives.

After the war Irene and Peter were finally married. They moved back to Irene's hometown, raised their family there and remained together all their lives. They are buried there alongside Irene's parents.

In 1995, Adolf and Maria Althoff were recognized by the Yad Vashem museum in Israel as 'Righteous Among the Nations', an honorary title bestowed on non-Jews who helped save the lives of Jewish people during the Holocaust.

There is so much history surrounding circus arts, that if I have whet your appetite with this general story of circus arts and the effect on trauma therapy in Ukraine, I urge you to continue to read, support and learn about the heritage of Ukraine.

Ukraine is a most intriguing and beautiful nation that I must believe will someday be free. It will open its borders and again welcome tourists without fear of missile, drones and rocket attacks attempting to destroy her, her people and her land.

CHAPTER 12

How to become a Circus Performer

When I began the research and discussion evolved about this story it was interesting fielding the questions from young people and friends. They wanted to know what they had to do to become a circus performer. Well, as a dancer/performer of some 27, years I had some ideas, but I went online to examine CareerExplorer, the world's leading career advancement platform. They research comprehensive questions with prospective students, before making predictions for that person. They have emerged with a high success rate.. *https://www.careerexplorer.com/* (accessed May 2025)

The following list is a brief outline of a possible process. It is not comprehensive or correct but will give you some ideas:

1. Get an education
2. Join a Circus school
3. Focus on a specific skill or act
4. Improve your physical fitness
5. Get an apprenticeship within a school or company
6. Get an act after training and practise it
7. Continue to build your skills and learn the art
8. Join a performance group or company...

The Indeed Editorial Team derived a very useful online article called 'How To Become a Circus Performer in 7 Steps (With Tips)' [https://www.indeed.com/career-advice/finding- a-job/how-to-become-circus-performer](https://www.indeed.com/career-advice/finding-a-job/how-to-become-circus-performer) (accessed May 2025)

The article provides a section called Writing an Effective Performer Resume (With Template and Examples) in addition to cover letters. The most pressing issue was

deciding what particular performer you wish to become. Some obvious suggestions are below, but these do not include many skills sets important to the circus actually

performing. These skills are related to the management, chorography, musicians and planning team.

- A trapeze artist
- Acrobat
- Daredevil
- Clown
- Dancer
- Singer
- In some parts of the world where still permitted, An animal trainer.

On the age-old tradition of animals being used in the programmes, it has become a serious stumbling block that is related to ethics and morality. Circus as a performing art is dependent on direct contact with the public, the spectator. Covid was disastrous during its breakout in 2019, and with the lack of direct contact and quarantine restrictions suspended circus activity. Circus can't be online.

Maintaining animals in confinement became critical but the biggest test was the Russian invasion of 2022. Morality is, as Romanenkova states, impossible to justify when using animals in experiments in zoos and circuses for entertainment or profit. She states that it is immoral to justify cruelty to animals for profit or benefit. It can be argued that the animals were born into such an existence. Thus, the decision to stop their inclusion created so many issues. It was unbalanced to make such an immediate action. This became a new dilemma irrespective of the war.

Where are these animals now, if not destroyed by the bombing? These decisions led to the inevitable physical death of perfectly healthy animals.

The material that is available apart from this article from 2022 no longer mention animals and so we can deduce that the performers are now predominantly human. (Romanenkova, 2022, p212)

CONCLUSION

'Circus is alive in Ukraine.'

This statement is a powerful phrase in two ways:

In its literal sense it refers to circus arts are still thriving in Ukraine.

There are schools, programmes, companies, performers and shows. Even during wartime. Ukraine will not be defeated and lose its heritage despite the invasion by Russia. Undeterred by the ongoing war and hardship. Ukrainian circus performers, companies, and schools have shown incredible resilience, continuing to perform, train, and even tour internationally. Defiant efforts such as these are morale-boosting for children and families.

In cities like Lviv, Dnipro, and even war-affected areas near Zaporizhzhia, mobile circus schools have been established.

Metaphorically speaking, circus in Ukraine is alive and well in spite of political and societal situations that are chaotic or surreal, because of the Russian invasion that should never have happened.

In a time when the world for many Ukrainian children has become a place of fear and unpredictability, the circus offers a counterbalance of laughter, rhythm, joy, community, and wonder.

It reminds them that their bodies can still move freely. That trust can be rebuilt. That stories -even painful ones - can be told with courage and colour. They can own their narrative and tell their story without words.

The circus is more than alive in Ukraine. It is saving lives, one laugh, one backflip, one unicycled smile at a time.

AUTHOR'S NOTE

I was born in Perth, Western Australia and raised as a typical Ukrainian child albeit in Western Australia. I was taught the language by my mother every evening and Ukrainian dancing at my father's Ukrainian Dancing School. I attended Ukrainian church at our Ukrainian Greek Catholic Church every Sunday and was required by my parents to attend most events for local Ukrainians at our Ukrainian Hall in Leederville. (now demolished to make way for a freeway extension)

Wherever there was a Ukrainian function my parents were either singing, cooking or organising for our community. Both parents had a deep and strong abiding love for the country they were forcibly taken from a young age, to be used as forced labourers by Hitler during WWII. They were unable to return to Ukraine at the end of the war as they would have faced execution by Stalin for being 'traitors.' They took advantage of Australia's post war refugee programme to begin a new life in peace and democracy, far removed from communism. They arrived in Perth in September 1950 aboard the Swedish Ship Skaugum 2.

At the time of writing this story in May 2025, my father had passed away 25 years ago but my amazing mother was still alive at 101 years of age.

Because of my heritage and formal education, I became an historian of the famine genocide in Ukraine during 1932-1933, The Holodomor.

The history of Ukrainian Migrant Refugees in Western Australia is documented in the subsequent publication that followed my thesis, 'Silent Memories - Traumatic Lives: Ukrainian Migrant Refugees in Western Australia.' (Melnyczuk, 2012)

The story of the Holodomor of 1932-1933 in Ukraine followed, with eyewitness accounts of the post-World War II refugees to Perth Western Australia being published. That book of narratives, the eyewitness accounts derived from my research, won an IPPY gold medal in the US. (Melnyczuk, 2018)

I began writing a series of children's books in 2021. I wanted to share my beloved Ukrainian heritage and customs through the eyes of five chickens, one newborn chick and two roosters. There will be a series of 10 books. The children's books are unique in that they also reflect community themes such as family, love, religion, respect for elderly, sibling support, the Holodomor intervention, helping those unable to help themselves, rare diseases in children, and bullying. The illustrations are inherently Ukrainian with each book concluding with interesting facts and activities for children to consider. They can be used with parental interaction or as a teaching tool. They are based for children from 4-10 years of age.

My research and my publications are my legacy for my parents, my children and my Ukrainian heritage. I publish under my Ukrainian name, Lesa Melnyczuk © 2025

Other Books By Lesa Melnyczuk featured on the following page.

OTHER BOOKS BY LESA MELNYCZUK

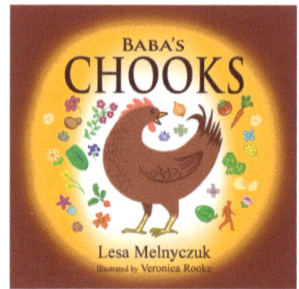
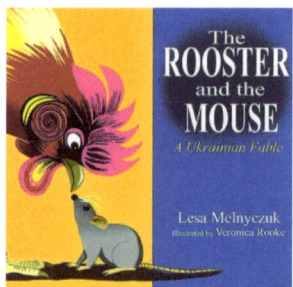
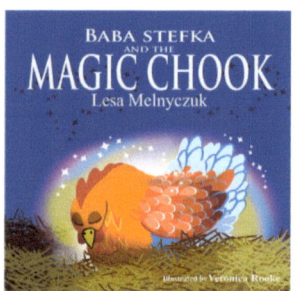
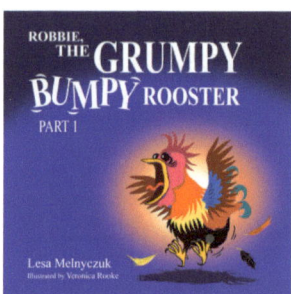
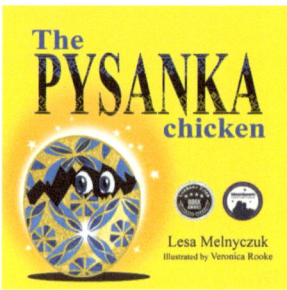
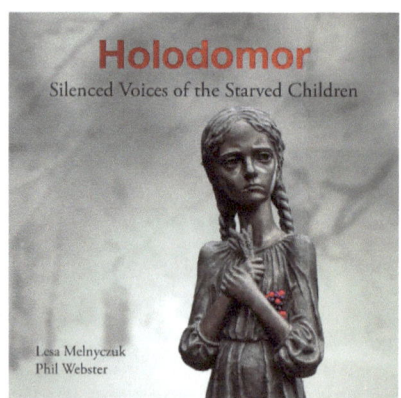
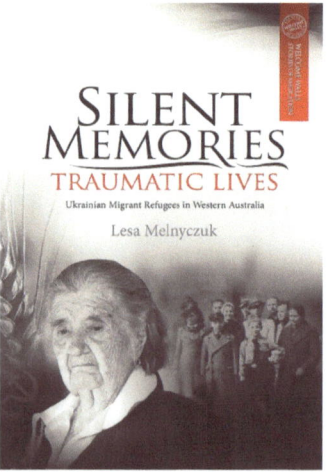

www.lesamelnyzuk.com

REFERENCES

ALMQVIST, K. and BROBERG, A. G. (1999) 'Mental Health and Social Adjustment in Young Refugee Children 3½ Years after Their Arrival in Sweden'. *Journal of the American Academy of Child & Adolescent Psychiatry* 38(6): 723–730.

BARBER, B. K. (2013) 'Annual Research Review: the Experience of Youth with Political Conflict—Challenging Notions of Resilience and Encouraging Research Refinement'. *Journal of Child Psychology and Psychiatry,* 54(4): 461–473.

BASSEL, L. (2005) Vive le Cirque! A French Initiative for Refugee Youth'. *Community Development Journal* 40(2): 232–235.

BERMAN, H. (2001) Children and War: Current Understandings and Future Directions'. *Public Health Nursing* 18(4): 243–252.

BESSONE, I. (2017) Social Circus as an Organized Cultural Encounter Embodied Knowledge, Trust and Creativity at Play'. *Journal of Intercultural Studies* 38(6): 651–664.

BETANCOUR, T. S. and WILLIAMS, T. W. (2008) Building an Evidence Base on Mental Health Interventions for Children Affected by Armed Conflict'. *Intervention* 6: 39–56.

BOLTON, R. (2004) Why Circus Works: How the Values and Structures of Circus Make It a Significant Developmental Experience for Young People'. Perth: *Murdoch University,* http://holisticcircustherapy.com/ufiles/pdfs/regphd.pdf (accessed October 2019).

'Building Resilience by Becoming a Circus Artist 783'. Journal of Refugee Studies, Vol34, Issue 1.March2021. https://academic.oup.com/jrs/article/34/1/760/5613786 (Downloaded on 03 May 2025).

BURROW, D. (2024) Circus in Ukraine – between a bright history and a difficult present. *https://www.scenic-circus.de/en/post/circus-in-ukraine-between-a-bright-history-and-a- difficult-present*

CALOINAU, Ioana, (2022) 'Review: Prague Circus brings together Czech and Ukrainian Performers'. Prague, *Expats cz* (Downloaded on 03 May 2025).

CARAVAN (n.d.) 'Framework of Competences for Social Circus Trainers', *http://www.caravan- circusnetwork.eu/wp-content/uploads/2015/02/LEO1fnalLOW2.pdf* (accessed August 2018).

CHERNOV DOCUMENTARY, (2010-2013)Ukraine, Kharkiv, Old Circus, Google, (accessed 14 April 2014)

CIRQUE DU SOLEIL, (n.d.) 'Social Circus Glossary of Cirque du Soleil', *http://www.cirkonet.cz/social-cirkus/online-odborne-publikace/download/4_37423bb61ba48eb990ad659213c2c610* (accessed October 2019).

CIRQUE DU SOLEIL, (n.d.). 'Cirque du Monde: Social Circus Program'. Retrieved from *https://www.cirquedusoleil.com/social-circus*

CIRQUE HORS PISTE, (2018). 'Social Circus and Trauma: Towards a Trauma-Informed Practice'. Montreal, Canada. Retrieved from *https://cirquehorspiste.com*

CLOWNS WITHOUT BORDERS USA. (n.d.). 'Our Work in Ukraine'. Retrieved from *https://clownswithoutborders.org/project/ukraine/*

COPELAND, K. A., KENDEIGH, C. A., SAELENS, B. E., KALKWARF, H. J. and SHERMAN, S. N. (2012) 'Physical Activity in Child-care Centers: Do Teachers Hold the Key to the Playground?'. *Health Education Research*, 27(1): 81–100.

DAUD, A., KLINTEBERG, B. and RYDELIUS, P. A. (2008) Resilience and Vulnerability among Refugee Children of Traumatized and Non-traumatized Parents'. *Child and Adolescent Psychiatry and Mental Health,* 2(1): 7.

DIMITRY, L. (2011) A Systematic Review on the Mental Health of Children and Adolescents in Areas of Armed Conflict in the Middle East'. *Child: Care, Health and Development,* 38: 153– 161.

DRIESSEN, H. G. G. M. and JANSEN, W. H. M. (2013) The Hard Work of Small Talk in Ethnographic Fieldwork'. *Journal of Anthropological Research,* 69(2): 249–264.

EHNTHOLT, K. A. and YULE, W. (2006) Practitioner Review: Assessment and Treatment of Refugee Children and Adolescents Who Have Experienced War-related Trauma'. 47(12): 1197–1210.

FALASCA, T. and CAULFIELD, T. J. (1999) Childhood Trauma'. *The Journal of Humanistic Counseling, Education and Development,* 37(4): 212–223.

FAZEL, M. and STEIN, A. (2002) The Mental Health of Refugee Children'. *Archives of Disease in Childhood*, 87(5): 366–370.

FOURNIER, C., DROUIN, M. A., MARCOUX, J., GAREL, P., BOCHUD, E., THE´ BERGE, J., AUBERTIN, P. L., FAVREAU, G. and FLEET, R. (2014) 'Cirque du Monde as a Health Intervention: Perceptions of Medical Students and Social Circus Experts'. *Canadian Family Physician*, 60: e548–e553.

FOX, P. G., BURNS, K. R., POPOVICH, J. M., BELKNAP, R. and FRANK-STROMBORG, M. (2004) 'Southeast Asian Refugee Children: Self-esteem as a Predictor of Depression and Scholastic Achievement in the U.S'. *International Journal of Psychiatric Nursing Research*, 9(2): 1063– 1072.

GELTMAN, P. L., GRANT-KNIGHT, W., MEHTA, S. D., LLOYD-TRAVAGLINI, C., LUSTIG, S., LANDGRAF, J. M. and WISE, P. H. (2005) 'The Lost Boys of Sudan: Functional and Behavioral Health of Unaccompanied Refugee Minors Resettled in the United States'. *Archives of Pediatrics & Adolescent Medicine,* 159(6): 585–591.

GIBBON, E., 1776. The History of the Decline and Fall of the Roman Empire, 1776, Chapter 31 - Games and spectacles, *http://www.ccel.org/ccel/gibbon/decline/files/volume1/chap31.htm#game*

GOTTLIEB, B. H. and BERGEN, A. E. (2010) Social Support Concepts and Measures'. *Journal of Psychosomatic Research*, 69(5): 511–520.

GOOGLE'S ENGLISH DICTIONARY, 2017. Google (accessed 2025)

HAMID, P. N. and LOK, D. P. P. (2000) 'Loneliness in Chinese Adolescents: A Comparison of Social Support and Interpersonal Trust in 13 to 19 Year Olds'. *International Journal of Adolescence and Youth,* 8(1): 45–63.

HIATT, B., 2025, *Perth Now*, Perth, The West Australia (Accessed 2 March 2025)

HONIS, Andrea, 2022, March 7. The Circus World Has United for Ukraine, Stage Lync newsletter. *https://stagelync.com/com/news/the-circus-world-has-united-for-ukraine*

KEKA¨LA¨INEN, K. (2014) Studying Social Circus—Openings and Perspectives. Finland: University of Tampere.

KYIV MUNICIPAL ACADEMY OF PERFORMING AND CIRCUS ARTS, n.d., *About the Academy*. (Retrieved from *http://example-url.ua*)

KINUNNEN, R., LIDMAN, J., KAKKO, S. C. and KEKALAINEN, K. (2013) They're Smiling from Ear to Ear': Wellbeing Effects from Social Circus'. Tampere: Centre for Practice as Research in Theatre, University of Tampere.

(KMACPA,11/04/2025) Municipal Academy of Performing and Circus Art... Wikipedia, *https://kmaecm.edu.ua/en/history*

KOBYLIANSKYI, M., 2025. Grikke from the air. Drone photograph.

KULEBA, Alina, (2024). 'Circus of Resilience: How Irpin's Studio Bounced Back from Wars'. Grip.Circus LifeNewsletter. *https://circuslife.com.ua/en/circus-of-resilience-how-irpin- studio-*...

LAFORTUNE, M. and BOUCHARD, A. (2011) Community Worker's Guide. When Circus Lessons Become Life Lessons'. *http://holisticcircustherapy.com/ufiles/library/Social_Circus_Guide.pdf* (accessed August 2019).

LOUGHRY, M., AGER, A., FLOURI, E., KHAMIS, V., AFANA, A. H. and QUOTA, S. (2006) 'The Impact of Structured Activities among Palestinian Children in a Time of Conflict'. *Journal of Child Psychology and Psychiatry* 47: 1211–1218.

LUSTIG, S. L., KIA-KEATING, M., KNIGHT, W. G., GELTMAN, P., ELLIS, H., KINZIE, J.D., KEANE, T. and SAXE, G. N. (2004) Review of: Child and Adolescent Refugee Mental Health'. *Journal of the American Academy of Child & Adolescent Psychiatry* 43(1): 24–36.784 Vera van Es et al. Downloaded from *https://academic.oup.com/jrs/article/34/1/760/5613786* 03 May 2025

MARSHALL, S. L., PARKER, P. D., CIARROCHI, J. and HEAVEN, P. C. L. (2014) Is Self- esteem a Cause or Consequence of Social Support? A 4-Year Longitudinal Study'. *Child Development* 85(3): 1275–1291.

MASON, D. (2014) Social Circus in a Warzone'. In Kekäläinen, K. (ed.) 'Studying Social Circus- Openings and Perspectives'. Finland: University of Tampere, pp. 14–23.

MCADAM-CRISP, J. L. (2006) Factors that Can Enhance and Limit Resilience for Children of War'. *Childhood* 13(4): 459–477.

MCCAFFERY, N. (2014) Social Circus and Applied Anthropology: A Synthesis Waiting to Happen'. *Anthropology in Action* 21(1): 30–35.

MCCAULEY, J. (2011) The Circus She Calls Me: Youth at Risk in a Social Circus', dare.uva.nl/ document/207817 (accessed October 2019).

MELNYCZUK, L (2012) Silent Memories - Traumatic Lives, Ukrainian Migrant Refugees in Western Australia. Perth, Western Australian Museum.

MELNYCZUK, L. (2018) Holodomor: Silenced Voices of the Starved Children. China, Carina Hoang Communications

MEYERSON, D. A., GRANT, K. E., SMITH CARTER, J. and KILMER, R. P. (2011) 'Posttraumatic Growth among Children and Adolescents: A Systematic Review'. *Clinical Psychology Review* 31(6): 949–964.

MILLER, K. E. (2004) Beyond the Frontstage: Trust, Access, and the Relational Context in Research with Refugee Communities'. *American Journal of Community Psychology* 33(3–4): 217–227.

MILLER, K. E. and RASCO, L. M. (2004) 'An Ecological Framework for Addressing the Mental Health Needs of Refugee Communities'. In Miller, K. E. and Rasco, L. M. (eds) *The Mental Health of Refugees: Ecological Approaches to Healing and Adaptation*. Mahwah, NJ: Lawrence Erlbaum Associates, Inc., pp. 1–64.

MORSE, J. M., BARRETT, M., MAYAN, M., OLSON, K. and SPIERS, J. (2002) 'Verification Strategies for Establishing Reliability and Validity in Qualitative Research'. *International Journal of Qualitative Methods* 1(2): 13–22. National Child Traumatic Stress Network (NCTSN). (2020). 'Early Childhood Trauma'. Retrieved from https://www.nctsn.org/what-is-child-trauma/trauma-types/early-childhood-trauma

NEWCOMB, M. D. and BENTLER, P. M. (1986) 'Loneliness and Social Support: A Confirmatory Hierarchical Analysis'. *Personality and Social Psychology Bulletin* 12(4): 520–535.

NICKERSON, A., BYRANT, R. A., ROSEBROCK, L. and LITZ, B. T. (2014) 'The Mechanisms of Psychosocial Injury following Human Rights Violations, Mass Trauma, and Torture'. *Clinical Psychology: Science and Practice* 21: 172–191.

ORTH, U. and ROBINS, R. W. (2014) The Development of Self-esteem'. *Current Directions in Psychological Science* 23(5): 381–38

PACIONE, L., MEASHAM, T. and ROUSSEAU, C. (2013) Refugee Children: Mental Health and Effective Interventions'. *Current Psychiatry Reports* 15(2): 341–349.

PANTER-BRICK, C., GRIMON, M. O., KALIN, M. and EGGERMAN, M. (2015) 'Trauma

Memories, Mental Health, and Resilience: A Prospective Study of Afghan Youth'. *Journal of Child Psychology and Psychiatry* 56(7): 814–825.

PAT-HORENCZYK, R., PELED, O., MIRON, T., BROM, D., VILLA, Y. and CHEMTOB, C. M. (2007) 'Risk-taking Behaviors among Israeli Adolescents Exposed to Recurrent Terrorism: Provoking Danger under Continuous Threat?'. *American Journal of Psychiatry* 164(1): 66–72.

PATTON, M. Q. (2002) Qualitative Research & Evaluation Methods. Thousand Oaks, London and New Delhi: SAGE Publications.

PELTONEN, K. and PUNAMÄKI, R. L. (2010) Preventive Interventions among Children Exposed to Trauma of Armed Conflict: A Literature Review'. *Aggressive Behavior* 36(2): 95–116.

PELTONEN, K., QOUTA, S., EL SARRAJ, E. and PUNAMÄKI, R. L. (2010) Military Trauma and Social Development: The Moderating and Mediating Roles of Peer and Sibling Relations in Mental Health'. *International Journal of Behavioral Development* 34(6): 554–563.

PERRY, B. D., & WINFREY, O. (2021). What happened to you? Conversations on trauma, resilience, and healing. NY, Flatiron Books.

PUNAMÄKI, R. L., QOUTA, S. and EL SARRAJ, E. (1997) Models of Traumatic Experiences and Children's Psychological Adjustment: The Roles of Perceived Parenting and the Children's Own Resources and Activity'. *Child Development* 68: 718–728.

ROMANENKOVA, Julia V. (2022) 'Ukrainian Traditional Circus in Today's Reality: between Formation and Abasement'. *ART Platform*. Kyiv, Research Gate.

ROTENBERG, K. J., MACDONALD, K. J. and KING, E. V. (2004) The Relationship between Loneliness and Interpersonal Trust during Middle Childhood'. *The Journal of Genetic Psychology* 165(3): 233–249.

RUBLE, Blaire A. (2025)

SAPIENZA, J. K. and MASTEN, A. S. (2011) 'Understanding and Promoting Resilience in Children and Youth'. *Current Opinion in Psychiatry* 24(4): 267–273.

SEYMOUR < Kristy Danialle (2012) How Circus Training Can Enhance the Well-being of Autistic Children and Their Families. Submitted in partial fulfilment of the requirements for the degree of Master of Arts and Media with Honours Griffiths, Creative Arts School of Humanities Griffith University. July 2012
https://ressources.cirquehorspiste.com/resources/2%20-%20Recherche%20en%20cirque%20social%20-%20Social%20circus%20research/2a%20-%20English/How%20circus%20can%20enhance%20the%20well-being%20of%20autistic%20children%20and%20their%20families.pdf

SHINN, M., LEHMANN, S. and WONG, N. W. (1984) Social Interaction and Social Support'. *Journal of Social Issues* 40(4): 55–76.

SIRKHANE SOCIAL CIRCUS SCHOOL: For Children, Inspired by Children, (n.d.) *https://www.sirkhane.org* (accessed 23 October 2019).

SPIEGEL, J. B. and PARENT, S. N. (2017) Reapproaching Community Development through the Arts: A Critical Mixed Methods Study of Social Circus in Quebec'. *Community Development Journal* 53: 600–617.

SPIEGEL, J. B., ORTIZ CHOUKROUN, B., CAMPAN˜ A, A., BOYDELL, K. M., BREILH, J. and YASSI, A. (2019) 'Social Transformations, Collective Health and Community-based Arts: "Buen Vivir'' and Ecuador's Social Circus Programme'. *Global Public Health* 14(6–7): 899– 922.

STRAUSER, D. R., LUSTIG, D. C., COGDAL, P. A. and URUK, A. C. (2006) Trauma Symptoms: Relationship with Career Thoughts, Vocational Identity, and Developmental Work Personality'. *The Career Development Quarterly* 54(4): 346 360.

SYDORENKO, Maksym (2024) 'Circus Across Continents: Ukrainian – Australian Perspective'. CircusLife Interviews: Episode#15.

TAYLOR, M. (2015) The Student Perception of Wellbeing Questionnaire: Preliminary Investigation into Its Psychometric Properties'. *International Journal of Disability, Development and Education* 62(1): 99–115.

TEDESCHI, R. G. and CALHOUN, L. G. (2004) 'Posttraumatic Growth: Conceptual Foundations and Empirical Evidence'. *Psychological Inquiry* 15(1): 1–18.

TOKUDA, Y., JIMBA, M., YANAI, H., FUJII, S. and INOGUCHI, T. (2008) 'Interpersonal Trust and Quality-of-life: A Cross-sectional Study in Japan'. *PLoS ONE* 3(12): e3985–e3994.

TOL, W. A., SONG, S. and JORDANS, M. J. D. (2013) 'Annual Research Review: Resilience and Mental Health in Children and Adolescents Living in Areas of Armed Conflict: A Systematic Review of Findings in Low- and Middle-income Countries'. *Journal of Child Psychology and Psychiatry* 54(4): 445–460.

TROTMAN, R. (2013) 'Evaluation of the SKIP Community Circus Programme in Dargaville', *http://www.communitycircus.co.nz/images/Research/Final%20SKIP%20Circus%20review% 20prog%20 evaluation%202013.pdf* (accessed August 2018).

UNICEF. (2014). Early childhood development in emergencies: Integrated programme guide. Retrieved from *https://www.unicef.org/media/107516/file/ECDE-Programme- Guide.pdf*

UNITED NATIONS HIGH COMMISSIONER FOR REFUGEES (2010) 'Convention and Protocol Relating to the Status of Refugees', *http://www.unhcr.org/protection/basic/3b66c2aa10/convention-protocolrelating-status- refugees.html* (accessed August 2018).

UNITED NATIONS HIGH COMMISSIONER FOR REFUGEES (2017) 'Global Trends: Forced Displacement in 2016', http://www.unhcr.org/statistics/unhcrstats/5943e8a34/global-trends-forced-displacement-2016.html (accessed August 2018).

VALENTINE ST LEON, 'Mark', 2010. The Dictionary of Sydney

VAN DER KOLK, B. A. (2014). The body keeps the score: Brain, mind, and body in the healing of trauma. NY., Viking.

VAN ES, Vera, ROMMES, Els, KWAADSTENIET, 'Leontien De',2021. *Journal of Refugee Studies*, Volume 34, Issue 1, March 2021, Pages 760–786, https://doi.org/10.1093/jrs/fez091Published: (accessed November 2019).

WARD, S. E. (2019). The art of the circus : An exploration of the circus within its social, historical, and cultural contexts. (Thesis). University of Hull. https://hull-repository.worktribe.com/output/4223574

WEINE, S. M. (2011) Developing Preventive Mental Health Interventions for Refugee Families in Resettlement'. *Family Process* 50(3): 410–430.

WEINE, S. M., DURRANI, A. and POLUTNIK, C. (2014) Using Mixed Methods to Build Knowledge of Refugee Mental Health'. *Intervention* 12: 61–77.

YU, X., LAU, J. T. F., ZHANG, J., MAK, W. W. S., CHOI, K. C., LUI, W. W. S., ZHANG, J. and CHAN,

E. Y. Y. (2010) 'Posttraumatic Growth and Reduced Suicidal Ideation among Adolescents at Month 1 after the Sichuan Earthquake'. *Journal of Affective Disorders* 123(1–3): 327–331.

 Lesa Melnyczuk is a Ukrainian, born in Australia. She began writing children's books after completing her PhD research, delving into the history of Ukraine during the early 1930's.

She likes to share a children's soft history of Ukraine and also traditions and fun stories through the words of Ukrainian Chickens and Ukrainian Babas, grandmothers.

The stories are about 5 amazing chooks all with Ukrainian names. They focus on love of elderly, family, brothers and sisters, care for birds and animals and children who may be sick, have special needs or have rare diseases.

Lesa's books telling Ukrainian stories through real events showing her deep connection to Ukrainian culture. They bring to life tales rich in tradition, emotion, and insight. Children become immersed in their narratives and experience the essence of Ukraine through the unique perspective of life in a chook pen on Baba Helen's property.

The first two books give children and introduction to the characters and then the fun begins.

The illustrations are simply magical. Children will imagine the characters of the chickens and children in the stories.

All human characters are have been taken from real people in Lesa's family, family life and events they have experienced. Children will find these stories believable and relatable.

Lesa is an award winning author for both Non Fiction (Holodomor) and children's books. Her personal reward is the joy or bringing a little bit of Ukraine into the lives of children from other cultures. Her books will be published in Ukrainian in the future for her Ukrainian speaking audience and diaspora.

Great books for children from any culture learning how to speak English and eventually, for children also learning how to speak Ukrainian.

For more information or to contact the author,
please visit: **www.lesamelnyczuk.com**

www.ingramcontent.com/pod-product-compliance
Lightning Source LLC
Chambersburg PA
CBHW041216070526
44583CB00001B/4